CHRISTIANITY
WORLD RELIGIONS

by Stephen F. Brown

Facts On File, Inc.

CHRISTIANITY
World Religions

Copyright © 1991 by Stephen F. Brown

Facts On File, Inc.
11 Penn Plaza
New York NY 10001

Library of Congress Cataloging-in-Publication Data

Brown, Stephen F.
   Christianity / by Stephen F. Brown.
      p. cm. — (World religions)
   Includes bibliographical references and index.
   Summary: Discusses the world's most widespread religion.
   ISBN 0-8160-2441-3
   1. Christianity — Juvenile literature. [1. Christianity.]   I. Title.   II. Series.
BR125.5.L96   1991
200 — dc20   90-25325

Developed by Brown Publishing Network, Inc.
Design Production by Jennifer Angell/Brown Publishing Network, Inc.
Photo Research by Nina Whitney
Photo credits:
Cover: Stained Glass Window from Bourges Cathedral, France,/Art Resource, NY.
Title page: **Adoration of the Kings,** Matteo di Giovanni,/The National Gallery, Washington, DC, from the Hamilton Collection, Mellon gift; Table of Contents page: Thirteenth-century French Crucifixion,/Bettmann Archive; *Pages 6-7* Skojld Photography; *9* Bettmann Archive; *10* AP/Wide World; *14* AP/Wide World; *16-17* Religious News Service; *24* Christ Teaching (**"La Petite Tombe"**), Rembrandt, etching/Art Resource; *29* **The Last Supper**, Leonardo da Vinci/Art Resource; *30* **The Crucifixion,** Piero della Francesca, painting/Bettmann Archive; *34-35* Religious News Service; *38* Bettmann Archive; *41* Catholic News Service; *44* Antonio Perez/ Catholic News Service; *46-47* AP/ Wide World; *60* Religious News Service; *63* UPI/Bettmann; *66* Art Resource; *69* UPI/ Bettmann; *72* Bettmann Archive; *76* Religious News Service; *78-79* Religious News Service; *83* Catholic News Service; *86* Ota Richter; *89* Catholic News Service; *92-93* Bettmann Archive; *95* J. Michael Fitzgerald/ Catholic News Service; *98* The Horn Book, Inc.; *99* Alinari/Art Resource; *103* Walters Art Gallery, Baltimore; *108* NC Picture Service/Catholic News Service; *110-111* Bettmann Archive; *119* AP/Wide World; *120* Catholic News Service.

Printed in the United States of America
RRD PKG 10 9 8 7 6 5
This book is printed on acid-free paper

TABLE OF CONTENTS

Preface

The 20th century is sometimes called a "secular age," meaning, in effect, that religion is not an especially important issue for most people. But there is much evidence to suggest that this is not true. In many societies, including the United States, religion and religious values shape the lives of millions of individuals and play a key role in politics and culture as well.

The World Religions series, of which this book is a part, is designed to appeal to both students and general readers. The books offer clear, accessible overviews of the major religious traditions and institutions of our time. Each volume in the series describes where a particular religion is practiced, its origins and history, its central beliefs and important rituals, and its contributions to world civilization. Carefully chosen photographs complement the text, and a glossary and bibliography are included to help readers gain a more complete understanding of the subject at hand.

Religious institutions and spirituality have always played a central role in world history. These books will help clarify what religion is all about and reveal both the similarities and differences in the great spiritual traditions practiced around the world today.

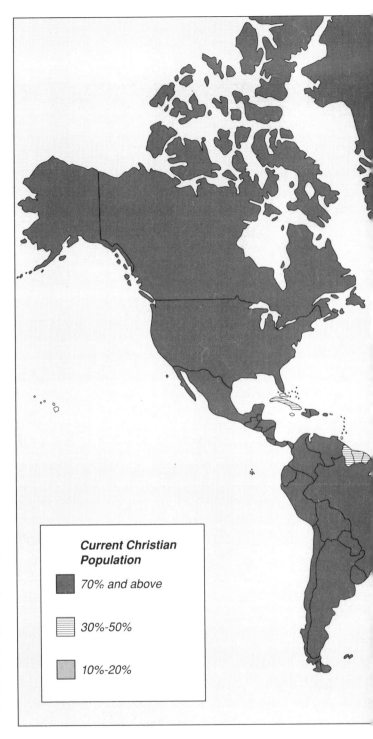

Current Christian Population

- 70% and above
- 30%-50%
- 10%-20%

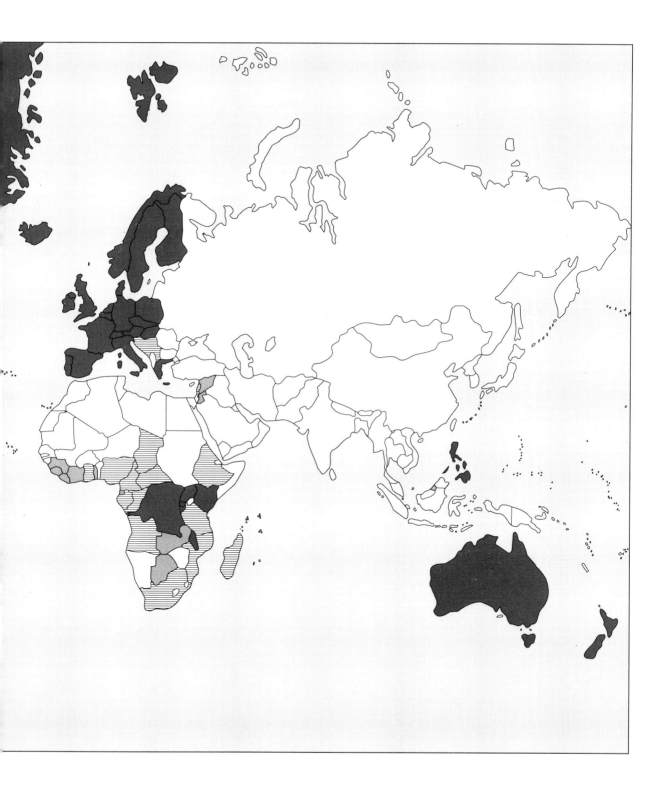

CHAPTER 1

Introduction: The Modern Christian World

$\mathbf{N}$orth America is a predominantly Christian continent. In fact, people born in present-day North America would find it hard to avoid the influence of the Christian religion. For example, the very year they were born would be the Year of our Lord 1940, or 1960, or 1980. Christmas, which celebrates Jesus Christ's birth, and Easter, which celebrates his rising from the dead, are among the most popular holidays on the North American continent. On a drive through almost any city or town in the United States or Canada, one is likely to see a towering cathedral, a high-steepled church in the center of town, or a simple meeting hall for Christian prayer. Turning on a television or a radio on any Sunday morning, one can hear a harmonious choir, a gospel singer, a preacher, or a quiet religious ceremony for the elderly, the sick or the disabled.

American history and culture have been shaped by Christianity in many ways. And the rich diversity of Christian faith is well suited for a nation of diverse peoples and traditions. The cathedral in your city might be Roman Catholic, Episcopalian, or Greek Orthodox. It might be called Saint Patrick's Cathedral, the

Cathedral of Saint John the Divine, or the Cathedral of Saint John of Damascus. Churches in your area might be called "First Congregational Church," "Berea Presbyterian Church," or "Calvary United Methodist Church." The notice board in front of a humble prayer hall might read "Middletown Believers Fellowship," "The Evangelical Friends Church," or "The Standard Church." Roman Catholic churches might be named after Saint Ludwig (German), Saint Brendan (Irish), Saint Anthony (Italian), Saint Louis (French), or Saint Theresa of Avila (Spanish). Despite common Christian beliefs and practices, there are many different Christian churches that have come to America's shores from many nations.

This Christian melting pot is not just a product of German, Irish, Italian, French, and Spanish immigrants. It consists of hundreds of Christian communities, some homegrown, some imported: Lutherans, Christian Scientists, Latter-day Saints, Independent Fundamentalists, Jehovah's Witnesses, Pentecostals, Unitarians, and Seventh-day Adventists. It is a Christian melting pot of people from England, France, and Germany; from Turkey and Greece; from Cuba, Haiti, and Argentina; from India and Taiwan. Christianity began in Palestine and over the centuries penetrated the cultures of every nation of the world. Christianity, in principle, is a religion of all nations. People from these many nations came to America's shores and brought their Christian faith with them. When they found it necessary, they even produced new, vital sects to express it.

The Universality of Christianity

Jesus Christ's command to his disciples was: "Go, teach all nations." According to the Christian Scriptures, God's chosen people before Jesus Christ were a particular people, the Jewish people. They, too, by their dedication to God's law and by their religious example, were meant to influence "the nations." According to Jewish law and the prophets, even as a particular nation they were meant, by God's plan, to spread God's care or concern for the world among their neighbors. Jesus Christ, however, by his interpretation of the Old Law and presentation of the New Law, released his followers from many of the customs that were followed by the Jewish people. Even more, he took the letter

 Many Protestant churches throughout small towns and rural areas of the United States and Canada are large bright halls of worship and prayer that focus on the study and preaching of the Bible.

of the Jewish law and gave it a spiritual interpretation that made it more universal.

In Matthew's Gospel, for example, Jesus Christ says:

Do not think that I have come to do away with the Law of Moses and the teachings of the prophets. I have not come to do away with them, but to make their teachings come true. . . .You have heard that people were told in the past, "Do not commit murder; anyone who does will be brought to trial." But now I tell you: whoever is angry with his brother will be brought to trial, whoever calls his brother "You good-for-nothing!" will be brought before the Council,

and whoever calls his brother a worthless fool will be in
danger of going to the fire of hell. (Matt. 5.17-22)

In spiritualizing the Mosaic Law, Jesus Christ extended the New Law to a world beyond the Jewish people. It is this more than spiritual law that one of his disciples, Paul, carried to the Mediterranean cities and towns outside of Palestine: to Galatia, Colossae, and Ephesus in Asia Minor, to Corinth, Thessalonica, and Philippi in Macedonia, and even to Rome.

The extension of the Christian religion beyond the Mediterranean basin to the whole world has taken many centuries, and in the Far East and in Muslim territories, its presence is still very small. Of the roughly 5 billion people in the world, however, more than 1.5 billion—33 percent of the world's population—are Christians.

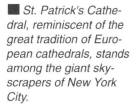 *St. Patrick's Cathedral, reminiscent of the great tradition of European cathedrals, stands among the giant skyscrapers of New York City.*

This universal extension can be seen in the large crowds that gather for Pope John Paul II's many trips to South America, Africa, and Asia. It can be viewed in the ecumenical missions of his Holiness Patriarch Dimitrios, archbishop of Constantinople, to the World Council of Churches, to the Vatican, and to the United States. This universal presence is also active in the large spiritual crusades of the Reverend Billy Graham in Helsinki, Tokyo, Seoul, or Rio de Janeiro.

On a more grand scale, however, the universal drive of Christianity can be seen in the growing numbers of Christians in Africa. Pope John Paul II's visits to this continent are very significant. He sees the future flourishing of Christian spiritual life to be much more promising in this world of poverty than in the materially prosperous nations of the West. Central and South America have Christian countries currently in political and religious upheaval. Roman Catholic, due to their faith and Spanish heritage, these nations are attempting to sort out their religious and political past, to untangle identities of religion and politics that have often allowed religion to be used by politicians for their own purposes. Vast populations of eastern Europe had been traditionally Catholic or Orthodox before the Communist suppressions of religion. There are already signs of significant resurgence of these faiths. Seminaries, or training schools for ministers and priests, are already growing at rapid pace in these formerly Communist-dominated countries.

The Far East is least populated by Christians but is seen as a very promising land for future Christian missionary work. Since the seventh century small communities of Christians in China, for example, have flourished, been suppressed, restored, and then persecuted again. A number of American Protestant churches have recently set up seminaries in California, the Philippines, and Korea, with the hope of spreading the gospel to the Oriental peoples. Even after almost 2000 years, Jesus Christ's command to "Preach to all nations" is still very much alive.

The Broad Nature of Christian Universality

The nature of this Christian universality is more than geographical. The Christian faith was meant by its founder to become part of every aspect of a believer's life. Therefore, it is not surprising that the Reverend Martin Luther King, Jr., led marches of Christians from every denomination for civil rights in the southern United States during the 1950s and 1960s. Nor is it unusual today for a Christian baseball player to make a sign of the cross before stepping to the plate or for a football star to kneel for a short, silent prayer of thanksgiving after scoring a touchdown. Neither is it strange to visit a sick relative at hospitals with names like Deaconess Hospital, New England Baptist Hospital, or Saint Mary's Hospital. It is almost expected that a soup kitchen for the poor or the homeless will be run by some church group. And paging through the phone book, one finds dozens of listings under the heading "Social Services" that reflect Christian origins.

Such examples are common in American life today. Yet many of the missions Americans assign to churches and church institutions are part of what they inherited from Europe, South America, and Canada. When those who came from England in the 19th century arrived here, they found churches that made them feel at home. The services were the same as in their homeland, and so were the hymns. If their Episcopalian descendants returned to England today, they would not feel like strangers in Anglican churches. The children of Lutherans who came from Germany were introduced to their religious traditions by the guidance of the General Synod, the General Council, and the United Synod South, which were fused into the United Lutheran Church in 1918. Lutherans today would feel quite comfortable if they returned for a service in an Evangelical church in the Germany of their forefathers. Celebrations of the feast of Saint Anthony in the North End of Boston, on Mott Street in New York, and on the streets of Cassino, Italy, have remarkable similarities. The blessing of the Portuguese fishing fleet would be as familiar to the people of Gloucester, Massachusetts, and Newport Beach, California, as to those of Lisbon or Oporto in Portugal or of Vitória or Santos in Brazil.

Likewise, French Canadians who poured into New England in the latter part of the 19th century brought with them their language and celebrations. A New England Catholic of French Canadian background would feel quite at home at the Church of

Notre Dame in Montreal or at the shrine of Sainte Anne de Beaupré, just outside Quebec.

The self-sacrificing character of Jesus Christ's gospel can be seen in the tireless efforts of Christians around the world. Mother Teresa, a Roman Catholic nun, is famous in all nations for her dedication to the poor and the sick of Calcutta. Bishop Desmond Tutu, an Episcopal Bishop, known for his courageous efforts to improve the lot of black South Africans, has been celebrated by an honorary degree from Harvard University. He is held in high esteem in many nations. Terry Waite, representing the Anglican Archbishop of Canterbury, attempted to negotiate a release of hostages being held in Lebanon which resulted in his own imprisonment.

Jesus Christ's words "Go, teach all nations" have been taken very seriously by his followers. In America, Catholics decided that it was important to build primary schools to pass on the teachings of Jesus Christ from generation to generation. Protestants, for the most part, used the public schools for primary education, since they could depend on their majority to influence school teaching policies. Christians generally, however, saw the need to develop Christian high schools, colleges, seminaries, and universities. Some of America's oldest and most highly regarded universities, such as Harvard and Yale, had religious origins. Duke, Emory, and Southern Methodist in the South; Boston College, Boston University, and Wesleyan in the Northeast; Earlham, Notre Dame, Loyola of Chicago, and Wheaton in the Midwest; Brigham Young, Pepperdine, and Seattle University in the West all have some Christian church affiliation.

These strong educational commitments in America follow from the seriousness given to education in the lands from which American immigrants came. Followers of Martin Luther brought into existence strong educational programs and university courses that still play a large part in German education. John Knox set high ideals for a comprehensive system of education that has strongly influenced Scotland and the Presbyterian Church. In the 16th, 17th, and 18th centuries in Italy and France, a large number of religious communities of women were formed that were dedicated to education. They continue to carry out their work in

Europe as well as in many religious schools in the United States and Canada. In the latter part of the 17th century, John Baptist de la Salle founded the Brothers of the Christian Schools, who today teach in Ireland, the United States, and Africa.

All these activities of the Christian churches show Christianity's vital presence throughout the world and in many areas of human endeavor—fighting for justice, healing the sick, clothing and feeding the poor, and visiting the imprisoned. Traditionally, these activities are the Christian works of mercy: feed the hungry, give drink to those who are thirsty, clothe the naked, shelter the homeless, ransom the captive, care for the sick, and bury the dead. In all these acts of charity and good will, the

Christian imagines that he sees Jesus Christ himself in the neighbor whom he helps. This act of imagination is based on the portrait of the Final Judgment in chapter 25 of the Gospel of Saint Matthew:

> *Then the King will say to the people on his right: "Come*
> *you that are blessed by my Father! Come and possess the*
> *kingdom which has been prepared for you ever since the*
> *creation of the world. I was hungry and you fed me, thirsty*
> *and you gave me a drink. I was a stranger and you received*
> *me in your homes, naked and you clothed me; I was sick*
> *and you took care of me, in prison and you visited me."*
> *The righteous will then answer him, "When, Lord, did we*
> *ever see you hungry and feed you, or thirsty and give you*
> *a drink? When did we ever see you a stranger and wel-*
> *come you in our homes, or naked and clothe you? When*
> *did we ever see you sick or in prison, and visit you?" The*
> *King will reply "I tell you, whenever you did this for one*
> *of the least important of these brothers of mine, you did*
> *it for me!"   (Matt. 25.31-46)*

The Christian Life: A Life of Prayer and Worship

For the Christian, all these visible activities that bear witness to Christianity's fruitfulness in today's world only have merit when they are performed out of love for God and one's neighbor. They are acts of praise to God for the glories of his creation, or acts of thanksgiving for God's benefits, or acts of love attempting to respond to the love that God has first shown to humankind, when, according to Christian belief, God's son "became flesh and dwelt amongst us." (John 1.14) The center of Christian life is not so much these activities themselves, but the life of prayer and worship that motivates the person in all areas of human endeavor.

This life of prayer and worship is shown in the high liturgical life of the Orthodox ceremonies, in the simple chant of the Benedictine monk, in the glorious choruses of the Mormon Tabernacle Choir, in the prayer services of the Methodist minister, in the vibrant "Amens" of the Pentecostals, in the quiet sittings of the Quakers.

CHAPTER 2

The Origins
of Christianity

*T*he Gospel of Matthew sets up many comparisons between Jesus of Nazareth and the New Law he offers and Moses and the Old Law he handed down to the Israelites. While presenting these differences, this Gospel also attempts to show how Jesus Christ continues the spirit of the Jewish law and fulfills the promises of the prophets. Matthew's Gospel thus cannot be fully understood without a knowledge of Judaism. In a sense, Matthew's Gospel is the Gospel associated with the Jewish Christian community. It introduces the reader to how the early Christian church in Jerusalem and its environs believed that Jesus, as the Son of God, brought a New Law that complemented the Old Law. It also explains how Jesus, as the Son of God, was the Messiah, or the anointed King promised to the Jewish people.

The Chosen People

To appreciate the Gospel of Matthew, then, one must go back to the beginnings of God's plan, as Christians understand it; one must go back to the Jewish Scriptures. According to the first book of the Jewish Scriptures, Genesis, the Hebrews descended from a

wandering herdsman, named Abram, who left Ur in Babylonia and, under God's guidance, went to Canaan. Through Abram, later called Abraham, the Lord God made a covenant with the Hebrew people. He promised them the land of Canaan and many descendants who would be kings. In Genesis, it is written that God promised Abraham that his descendants would become a mighty nation.

> *Now the Lord said to Abram, "Go from your country and your kindred and your father's house to the land that I will show you. And I will make of you a great nation, and I will bless you, and make your name great, so that you will be a blessing. I will bless those who bless you, and him who curses you I will curse, and by you all the families of the earth shall bless themselves." (Gen. 12.1-3)*

Abraham's wife, Sarah, however, was old and unable to have children, so his trust in God's promise of many descendants was being tested. Sarah told Abraham to have a child through her servant Hagar, and he did have a son whom he named Ishmael. But God, Genesis tells us, scolded Sarah and Abraham and told them they must have trust in him. Finally, as God had said, Abraham had a son by Sarah, and the son was named Isaac. But, once again, the Genesis story declares, God tested Abraham and asked him to sacrifice Isaac. Abraham wondered how he could have descendents that would become a great nation if he sacrificed his wife's son, Isaac. Abraham showed his trust in God and obeyed; and at the last minute Isaac was saved by the cry of an angel telling him not to lay his hand on the boy. Abraham thus became known in the Jewish and Christian traditions as the father of faith, the father of trust.

Abraham's descendants multiplied, but after many years they found themselves captives in Egypt. Again, Genesis continues, God's care for his people showed through. He helped them escape from Egypt and guided them to the promised land. On the way, according to the Book of Exodus, God renewed his agreement with the descendants of Abraham, by giving Moses and his people the Ten Commandments and other laws and by renewing his promise to watch over them as his chosen people.

> ■ **The Ten Commandments**
>
> **I.** *I am the Lord your God, who brought you out of the land of Egypt, out of the house of bondage. You shall have no other gods before me.*
>
> **II.** *You shall not take the name of the Lord your God in vain.*
>
> **III.** *Observe the sabbath day, to keep it holy.*
>
> **IV.** *Honor your father and your mother.*
>
> **V.** *You shall not kill.*
>
> **VI.** *Neither shall you commit adultery.*
>
> **VII.** *Neither shall you steal.*
>
> **VIII.** *Neither shall you bear false witness against your neighbor.*
>
> **IX.** *Neither shall you covet your neighbor's wife.*
>
> **X.** *You shall not desire your neighbor's house, his field, or anything that is your neighbor's.*

According to Jewish history, the chosen people entered the promised land and some of Abraham's descendants became kings; of these, David and Solomon were the most famous. The kingdom split into Israel and Judah, and each in turn was captured by the Assyrians and the Babylonians. The descendants of Abraham and David frequently found themselves dominated by foreign nations. They felt especially dominated, Jewish historians tell us, by the ruler Antiochus Epiphanes, who sacrificed a pig in their temple as an act of ridicule. This caused a revolt that is commemorated by the Hanukkah holiday—the celebration of the reconsecration of the temple in 165 B.C.

These frequent dominations of the Jewish people, from the time of the Assyrian captivity (about 731 B.C.) to the time of the Maccabees (about 165 B.C.), Jewish prophets tell us, helped build a hope for a new leader who might free them from slavery. In these years before Jesus Christ's birth the prophets, starting with Isaiah, foretold the coming of a Messiah, a savior who would redeem his people and restore the kingdom. The Messiah was pictured in different ways by Jewish writers: some thought he would return as a military leader overthrowing their oppressors;

others expected him to be a great teacher; still others imagined him, according to the prophecy of Jeremiah, as a suffering servant.

Jesus the Messiah

Matthew's Gospel presents Jesus Christ as a descendant of Abraham and David. Jesus is thus presented, like Abraham, as one from whom a great nation would descend. He is also, like David, a king who can lead his people.

The very beginning of this Gospel, then, recalls the hopes held so high among the oppressed Jewish people. It was during these days of high expectations for a Messiah that a man began to go among the Jewish people and preach about the coming of the kingdom of heaven:

The kingdom of heaven is like a grain of mustard seed which a man took and sowed in his field; it is the smallest of all seeds, but when it has grown it is the greatest of shrubs and becomes a tree, so that the birds of the air come and make nests in its branches. (Matt. 13.31-32)

With such stories or parables this man instructed the expectant Jewish people about the kingdom of his Father:

Our Father, who art in heaven, Hallowed be thy name. Thy kingdom come. Thy will be done on earth as it is in heaven. Give us this day our daily bread. And forgive us our debts, as we forgive our debtors. And lead us not into temptation, but deliver us from evil: For thine is the kingdom, and the power, and the glory, for ever. Amen. (Matt. 6.9-13)

Some saw this wandering preacher as merely another of the great rabbis, or teachers, who spent their days interpreting and reshaping Jewish law. Others saw him as a leader in their fight against Roman rule. And some saw him as the Messiah, sent by God to deliver them. This man was a carpenter named Jesus of Nazareth.

For hundreds of years, historians and theologians have been searching for evidence of the historical existence of Jesus of Nazareth. Today, it is generally accepted that he did in fact live.

The principal source of information about his life is the New Testament of the Christian Bible, especially the Gospels of Matthew, Mark, Luke, and John.

Stories about Jesus Christ and what were believed to be his sayings circulated first by word of mouth and were later collected and written down. It was from such oral and written sources that the four Gospels were compiled. The first of these, the Gospel of Mark, was written in about A. D. 62, only thirty years after the death of Jesus. Written so soon after the events they describe, these books present a strong body of evidence of the existence of Jesus. Here is the story they tell.

Sometime around the year 6 B.C., the Roman Emperor Augustus Caesar ordered a census to be taken of all the people of the empire. The purpose of the census was to register men for service in the Roman army and to ensure the accuracy of population figures for tax collection purposes.

Because the census required that each man be registered in the town of his birth, a carpenter named Joseph made the long, difficult journey from Nazareth in Galilee to Bethlehem in Judea, where he had been born. His pregnant wife, Mary, accompanied him.

When they arrived in Bethlehem, the travelers were turned away from an inn for lack of room. As the Gospel of Luke tells us, they were forced to seek shelter in a stable, where Mary "gave birth to her first-born son and wrapped him in swaddling clothes, and laid him in a manger." (Luke 2.7) Mary and Joseph named their child Joshua, which in Hebrew means "God is salvation." The Greeks made this into *Iesous*, the Romans into *Iesus*, or Jesus.

The Gospel of Matthew (2. 1-12) relates the events surrounding the birth of Jesus:

> *After Jesus' birth in Bethlehem of Judea during the reign of King Herod, astrologers from the east arrived one day in Jerusalem, inquiring, "Where is the newborn king of the Jews? We observed his star at its rising and have come to pay him homage." At this news King Herod became greatly disturbed, and with him all Jerusalem. Summoning all of the chief priests and scribes of the*

people, he inquired of them where the Messiah was to be born. "In Bethlehem of Judea," they informed him. Here is what the prophet has written: "And you, Bethlehem, land of Judah, are by no means least among the princes of Judah, since from you shall come a ruler who is to shepherd my people to Israel." Herod called the astrologers aside and found out from them the exact time of the star's appearance. Then he sent them to Bethlehem, after having instructed them: "Go and get detailed information about the child. When you have found him, report it to me so that I may go and offer him homage too." After their audience with the king, they set out. The star which they had observed at its rising went ahead of them until it came to a standstill over the place where the child was. They were overjoyed at seeing the star, and on entering the house, found the child with Mary his mother. Then they opened their coffers and presented him with gifts of gold, frankincense, and myrrh. They received a message in a dream not to return to Herod, so they went back to their country by another route.

In truth, Herod had no intention of worshiping a child proclaimed as the newborn king of the Jews. Herod had become increasingly angered by the talk throughout his kingdom of the coming of the Messiah. When he heard the reports of the astrologers—who were probably learned men from Babylon or Persia—that a child had been born in Bethlehem who was to be the king of the Jews, he flew into a rage. Fearing that his position as King of Judea was threatened, he ordered his soldiers to kill all male children under two years of age in the region of Bethlehem.

Forewarned in a dream of the impending slaughter of the innocents, Joseph fled with his family to Egypt. Soon afterward, Herod died. When news of the king's death reached Egypt, Joseph and his family returned to their home in Nazareth.

Little is known about the childhood of Jesus. However, we can assume that, as was the custom of his time and place, he began to work alongside Joseph at an early age and learned the trade of carpenter. And because he was Jewish, we can also assume that he learned the ritual requirements of Jewish law and memorized verses of the Bible. We are told that although he could read and write, he had no formal education, because, according to the Gospels of Mark and John, his neighbors asked: "How is it that this man can read when he has never gone to school?"

The only incident of Jesus' childhood that the Gospels record is his meeting with the rabbis, or teachers, of the Temple in Jerusalem when he as twelve years old. According to Luke, Jesus' knowledge and understanding of Jewish law astonished and impressed the rabbis.

About A.D. 26 or 27, a man called John the Baptist began a new religious movement, preaching to the people about the coming of the Messiah and urging them to repent their sins and live a just life. Throughout history, many different peoples have believed there is a mystical power in flowing water that can cleanse people of their sins. And so before he preached, John baptized people by immersing them in the water of the River Jordan. Jesus was one of the many who went to John to be baptized. According to the Gospel of Mark (1.12), Jesus went into the wilderness immediately after his baptism, where he remained for forty days. During this time, Jesus may have begun to realize that he was the Messiah about whom John was preaching, although at no time did he proclaim himself to be the Messiah.

Following John's arrest and imprisonment by Herod Antipas, tetrach of Galilee, Jesus took up John the Baptist's work and began his own ministry, preaching a similar message.

Jesus' method was to go to the people, especially the common people. He was a Jew, preaching to other Jews. In the synagogue on the Sabbath, learned men were often called upon to speak during the service, and it is likely that this is where Jesus first began to preach, before the crowds who listened to him grew too large. As his following increased, he taught on the streets and roads, by the sea, and in the countryside—wherever he found people to hear his message.

Jesus' central theme was the kingdom of heaven (or the kingdom of God, which means the same thing). He strove to prepare his people for the coming of the kingdom of God and for the Last Judgment, when all people would be judged by God

Jesus Christ, teaching in the temple, is portrayed in this etching by the Dutch artist, Rembrandt.

according to their actions here on earth. Because of the sinfulness of humanity, it was necessary for them to take up a new life of obedience in fellowship with others who were also waiting for God to establish his kingdom on earth.

Jesus taught that salvation depends on true devotion to the will of God, not merely following the letter of religious law. In his sermons and parables, or stories that illustrate a religious principle, Jesus drew from Judaic tradition for the message of love and forgiveness that he preached, but he gave new meaning to this tradition. The essential difference between his teachings and the teachings of Judaism was the emphasis on *love* as opposed to *law*. Jesus called people away from the letter of the Jewish law to its spirit. He did not think that he was overthrowing Judaic law—he said, "I came not to destroy the Law of Moses but to fulfill it." (Matt. 5. 17) Nevertheless, his teachings created enemies among the religious leaders whose authority he was undermining. He was growing into a Jewish leader with a large following.

Jesus as the New Lawgiver

In chapter 5 of his gospel, Matthew recounts the Sermon on the Mount. This sermon, like Moses' reception of the Ten Commandments, takes place on a mountain. It provides the teachings of the New Law or Covenant:

> *Blessed are the poor in spirit, for theirs is the kingdom of heaven. Blessed are those who mourn, for they shall be comforted. Blessed are the meek, for they shall inherit the earth. Blessed are those who hunger and thirst for righteousness, for they shall be satisfied. Blessed are the merciful, for they shall obtain mercy. Blessed are the pure in heart, for they shall see God. Blessed are the peacemakers, for they shall be called sons of God. Blessed are those who are persecuted for righteousness' sake, for theirs is the kingdom of heaven.   (Matt. 5.3-10)*

Jesus then goes on to compare the Law and the gospel teaching:

> *I tell you, then, that you will be able to enter the Kingdom of heaven only if you are more faithful than the teachers of the Law and the Pharisees in doing what God requires.*

Moses, according to Matthew's account, had received the Old Law from God; Jesus proclaims the New Law as God: "You have heard it said. . . but now I tell you. . . . It was also said. . .but now I tell you. . . . When you give something to a needy person, do not make a big show of it. . . . When you pray, do not be like the hypocrites. . . ."(Matt. 5.20 - 6.2)

In Matthew's Gospel, Jesus speaks as a Lawgiver. He speaks with divine authority.

Jesus' first followers were simple people, like Peter and Andrew who were fishermen and Matthew who was a tax collector.

They traveled with him through Galilee and to Jerusalem as he taught the crowds, his message usually presented in parables.

> *Once there was a man who went out to sow grain. As he scattered the seed in the field, some of it fell along the path, and the birds came and ate it up. Some of it fell on rocky ground, where there was little soil. The seeds soon sprouted, because the soil wasn't deep. But when the sun came up, it burned the young plants; and because the roots had not grown deep enough, the plants soon dried up. Some of the seeds fell among thorn bushes, which grew up and choked the plants. But some seeds fell in good soil, and the plants bore grain: some had one hundred grains, others sixty, and others thirty. (Matt. 13.18-23)*

Such simple stories had profound meanings, and Jesus, Matthew tells us, unraveled their mystery for his disciples:

> *Those who hear the message about the Kingdom but do not understand it are like the seeds that fell along the path. The Evil One comes and snatches away what was sown in them. The seeds that fell on rocky ground stand for those who receive the message gladly as soon as they hear it. But it does not sink deep into them, and they don't last long. So, when trouble or persecution comes because of the message, they give up at once. The seeds that fell among thorn bushes stand for those who hear the message; but the worries about this life and the love for riches choke the message, and they don't bear fruit. And the seeds sown in the good soil stand for those who hear the message and understand it: they bear fruit, some as much as one hundred, others sixty, and others thirty.*

The Pharisees, with their abiding concern for the traditional interpretation of the Mosaic Law or Law of Moses, challenged Jesus and planned to entrap him with their questions. Jesus, however, showed that he knew the Law and the prophets better than they. As Matthew indicates: "And from that day on no one dared to ask him any more questions." (Matt. 22.46)

■ Books of the New Testament

Gospels—Matthew, Mark, Luke, John
Acts of the Apostles
Letters
Romans
1 Corinthians
2 Corinthians
Galatians
Ephesians
Philippians
Colossians
1 Thessalonians
2 Thessalonians
1 Timothy
2 Timothy
Titus
Philemon
Hebrews
James
1 Peter
2 Peter
1 John
2 John
3 John
Jude
Revelation

Jesus as Suffering Servant

John the Baptist had paid with his life for preaching in Judea. Jesus decided to go there himself to preach, even though he knew this would be dangerous.

In the spring of the third year of his ministry, Jesus traveled from Galilee to Jerusalem for Passover. We have no portrait of Jesus made while he lived, but we can picture him in the dress of other men of that time and place, long-haired and bearded, wearing a tunic under a cloak and sandals on his feet. To shield him from the sun, he probably wore a cloth headdress falling over his shoulders. According to Matthew's Gospel (21. 8-11), his entry into the city was triumphal, with crowds of people proclaiming him the Messiah. In the traditional eastern manner, many honored him by throwing their cloaks in front of him, and others cut branches from trees and strewed them in his path.

As soon as Jesus' presence in Jerusalem became known to the priests of the Temple, they began plotting against him. Jesus' greatest enemies were the Pharisees and scribes, members of a learned class who studied the scriptures and served as copyists, editors, teachers, and jurists. These religious leaders demanded that people conform not only to the written law as handed down by Moses but also to the developed oral tradition that applied it. Jesus' readiness to disregard ceremonial rules and oral tradition to meet human need, as well as his emphasis on the human, the spiritual, and the moral rather than on the legal or ritual, challenged their way of life. They became actively hostile to him.

Once inside the walls of Jerusalem, Jesus made his way to the magnificent Temple that had been built by Herod the Great. The Temple, which should have been a holy place, was noisy, crowded, and dominated by the selling of sacrificial doves and animals. Money-changers shouted the rates they would give to exchange the currencies used in the various parts of the land for the silver money of Jerusalem. Pilgrims, coming to worship Yahweh, moved among the merchants and money-changers, haggling over the price to be paid. Enraged by this irreverence, Jesus overturned the tables of the money-changers and drove the merchants from the Temple, shouting, "Make not God's house a marketplace!" Through this act, he made enemies of the Sadducees, who controlled the Temple worship. They added their opposition to that of the Pharisees.

Perhaps because he sensed the danger that surrounded him, Jesus slept outside the city walls. However, he returned daily to the crowded Temple to preach the message that so enraged the Pharisees. Jesus' followers could not understand his forebodings. Secretly they believed that during the Passover celebrations, Jesus would reveal himself as the Messiah.

The night before the beginning of Passover, Jesus and his twelve disciples gathered in the house of one of his followers to have supper together. Before the meal, in an act of humility, Jesus washed his disciples' feet, saying to them, "Now I have given you an example that you should do as I have done. Remember, the servant is not greater than his lord; neither is he that is sent greater than he that sent him." (John 13. 15-16)

It was at this meal that Jesus spoke the words that serve as the basis for the Christian sacrament of Holy Communion, in which bread and wine are partaken of in commemoration of the death of Christ. Jesus took bread and when he had given thanks, broke it and shared it with his disciples, saying, "This is my body which is for you. Do this in remembrance of me." Then he blessed the wine that he gave his disciples to drink and said, "This cup is the new covenant in my blood. Do this, as often as you drink it, in remembrance of me." (I Corinth. 11. 24-25)

During the course of the meal, Jesus suddenly said, "Verily I say to you that one of you shall betray me." He did not identify the traitor, saying only, "It is one of the twelve that eateth with me," and adding, "It were better for my betrayer were he never born."

When the meal was over, Jesus told his disciples, "Children, I shall be with you only a little while longer. Ye shall seek me, but whither I go you cannot come. So now I say to you: A new commandment I give unto you, that you love one another. As I have loved you, so you shall love one another. By this shall all know that you are my disciples—if you have love for one another." (John 13. 34-35)

After the Last Supper, Jesus withdrew into a garden called Gethsemane, where he often went for prayer and meditation. His

---

■ The Twelve Apostles or Disciples of Christ

Peter
Andrew
James
John
Philip
Bartholomew
Matthew
Thomas
James the son of
   Alphaeus
Simon the Zealot
Judas the son of James
Judas Iscariot

disciples went with him, save for Judas, who had left them earlier in the evening. As his disciples slept around him, Jesus prayed.

Late at night, the silence of the garden was broken by the arrival of Judas, leading a band of Roman soldiers and Jewish Temple police. Identified by the betraying kiss of Judas, Jesus was arrested and brought before the Sanhedrin, the council of Jewish leaders. After an irregular trial, the Sanhedrin found Jesus guilty of blasphemy. By Roman law, however, the Sanhedrin could not put Jesus to death. In order to avoid arousing the anger of Jesus' followers and to ensure his death, they took him before Pontius Pilate, the Roman procurator, and charged him with blasphemy and with organizing a revolt against Rome.

Pilate found Jesus innocent of treason and wanted to set him free. The Pharisees, however, would not let Pilate release him. Perhaps in an attempt to stay out of the internal conflicts among the Jews, Pilate gave in and sentenced him to death. As was the custom with all condemned criminals, Jesus was first scourged,

■ Leonardo Da Vinci's **The Last Supper** portrays Jesus Christ's final meal with his disciples before his crucifixion and death.

or whipped, and the mocking soldiers placed a crown of thorns on his head.

Guarded by soldiers and followed by a curious mob, Jesus and two thieves who had also been sentenced to die that day were lead to a hill outside Jerusalem called Golgotha. Weak from loss of blood and lack of sleep, Jesus stumbled along, carrying on his back, as was the custom, the cross on which he was to be executed. He was followed by a great crowd of people, many of whom beat their fists upon their breasts and wept openly.

Crucifixion was the form of death reserved by the Romans for low criminals, slaves, and revolutionaries. After Jesus' death, his followers believed that his crucifixion was the fulfillment of a prophecy of Isaiah's that the Messiah would be "despised and rejected of men, a man of sorrows and acquainted with grief.... Surely he has borne our griefs, and carried our sorrows....he was wounded for our transgressions, bruised for our iniquities...and

■ *The Crucifixion,* painted by Piero della Francesca, shows the final hours of Christ's life. The crucifixion scene is recounted in each of the four gospels (Matthew, Mark, Luke, and John).

with his stripes we are healed. The Lord hath laid upon him the iniquity of us all.... He was taken from prison and from judgment, and was cut off out of the land of the living." (Isaiah 53. 4-8) A sign that Pontius Pilate ordered nailed to Jesus' cross provided more fuel for the ridicule of those who did not believe in Jesus as the Messiah: "Jesus of Nazareth, King of the Jews," it said in Aramaic, Greek, and Latin. (John 19.19-20)

When the soldiers and the mob taunted the dying Jesus, he whispered, "Father, forgive them for they know not what they do." After hours of unbearable pain, he cried out, "My God, my God, why hast thou forsaken me?" Then his head dropped onto his chest, and it was over.

A Roman officer reported to Pilate that Jesus was dead, and his body was turned over to one of his followers, Joseph of Arimathea, for burial. Jesus' body was wrapped in a linen shroud and placed in a tomb that was sealed with a rock.

The Resurrection of Jesus

According to Matthew's Gospel, on the third day after Jesus was crucified, Mary Magdalene and the other Mary, the mother of James and Joseph, went to look at the tomb. There was a violent earthquake and an angel spoke to the women: "You must not be afraid. I know that you are looking for Jesus, who was crucified. He is not here. He has been raised, just as he said. Come here and see the place where he was lying." (Matt. 28. 6)

Later, the Gospel says, Christ appeared to the eleven disciples. He said to them: "I have been given all authority in heaven and on earth. Go, then, to all peoples everywhere and make them my disciples: baptize them in the name of the Father, the Son, and the Holy Spirit, and teach them to obey everything I have commanded you. And I will be with you always, to the end of the world." (Matt. 28.18-20) With these words, the story of Jesus according to Matthew's Gospel ends. Yet, according to Christian belief, Christ continued, and continues, to live through his church.

The Early Christian Church

The first Christians were the disciples of Christ, the simple fishermen that he wanted to make fishers of men. Their first "catch," according to the Acts of the Apostles, was the Jewish community that had heard him preach, saw the wonders he performed, and saw in him a great prophet and then more than a prophet. The early origins of the Christian church are hardly distinguishable from a special Jewish community. Many Jews saw Christ as a special rabbi, a special teacher. Only gradually did they come to believe that Christ was more than just a teacher and that he had a larger mission. At first, they continued to perform all the Jewish rituals on the Sabbath. Little by little they reenacted the Passover meal with its new meaning, realizing that Christ had by his death and resurrection given it a new reality. As the fuller meaning of Christ's life and teaching dawned on them, Christian historians tell us, they began to separate from the temple and synagogue. They also gradually became suspect by the Jewish communities who began to eject them from the Jewish houses of prayer and worship. It is this stage of development that is chronicled in the Gospel of Matthew.

Christians believe that Christ was a teacher, but one who gave a New Law in his own name, thereby indicating that he was God. When he spoke of God as his Father, he spoke, according to Christian believers, as one equal to his Father. They believed that his teachings gave a whole new meaning to the Old Law, and his death was a sacrifice that replaced all the sacrifices of the Old Law. His resurrection, according to Christian faith, was a guarantee to his claims and of his promises. These claims also called for believers to have the same kind of unwavering faith in God as Abraham had. Christ called not just for obedience to a law; he called for a new faith that believed the new meanings and the new vision he brought to human life. These themes of the Jewish community of Christians, sounded in Matthew's Gospel, also are the themes of Paul's Epistle to the Hebrews. Both these writings put us in touch with the first community of Christians—the Jewish community of Christians.

The Gospel Preached to the Gentiles

Paul, a convert to Christianity from Judaism and a key writer of the New Testament, may have preached and written to the Hebrews, but it is not for that work that he is best known. As he tells us in his Letter to the Galatians, a Gentile (non-Jewish) people to whom he had preached about Christ, he had been a very fervent Jew. He studied under the great rabbi Gamaliel. He even persecuted the Christians and was present at the death of the first Christian martyr, Stephen. However, God brought him to a dramatic conversion, he claims, and Saul of Tarsus became Paul, the Apostle to the Gentiles. His letters to the many Christian communities show a man of tireless energy and daring adventures. His journeys are recounted in the Acts of the Apostles, chapters 13-28.

One of his most stirring letters is the Epistle to the Galatians. It reveals the tensions of the early Christian church, so anchored in Jewish tradition and encountering a world that is not Jewish. Some Judaizers, those favoring a more Jewish form of Christianity, had come to Galatia after Paul had preached there, and they had preached a more Jewish form of Christianity. According to them, to become a Christian one must first become circumcised like a Jew. In this Epistle, Paul mocks these preachers, portraying them as preachers of "another gospel." If the Galatians follow these false preachers, faith in Christ and his redeeming sacrifice, Paul argues, is being betrayed in favor of salvation by following the demands of the Mosaic Law. For Paul, it is no longer the Old Law that saves; it is faith in Christ's life and death that saves and brings to the Christian such fruits of faith as charity, joy, peace, patience, kindness, goodness, humility, self-control, and faithfulness itself. These are the gifts of the Spirit, Paul declares, that should direct their lives. They are not the results of following the Mosaic Law. Christians are saved, Paul contends, not through the Law, but through Christ. Christians must say: "I am not saved by the works of the Law. I have been put to death with Christ on his Cross, so that it is no longer I who live, but it is Christ who lives in me. This life that I live now, I live by faith in the Son of God, who loved me and gave his life for me." (Gal. 2.19-20) After much dispute with those who wanted to preserve the Christian ties with the Jewish tradition, Paul's argument triumphed over the Judaizers and paved the road to a universal Christianity, free from the burdens of the Mosaic Law.

CHAPTER 3

The History
of Christianity

Christians believe that the birth of the church took place when Jesus sent the Holy Spirit to guide his apostles on Pentecost Sunday, which is fifty days after Jesus Christ's resurrection. Forty days after Christ's resurrection from the dead, he ascended into heaven. According to the Acts of the Apostles, Christ's ascension, 10 days before Pentecost, left his disciples lonely and confused. The closing words of Matthew's Gospel make clear what Christ had promised his followers: "I am with you always, to the close of the age." (Matt. 28.20) Yet, he had seemingly left them to themselves. The Acts of the Apostles describes the disciples' sense of loss, their feeling that Christ had deserted them, and how they huddled together in fear and bewilderment. As they hid away:

> *Suddenly there came a sound from heaven as of a rushing mighty wind, and it filled all the house where they were sitting. And there appeared unto them cloven tongues like as of fire, and they sat upon each of them. And they were all filled with the Holy Spirit, and began to speak with other tongues, as the Spirit gave them utterance.* (Acts 2.2-4)

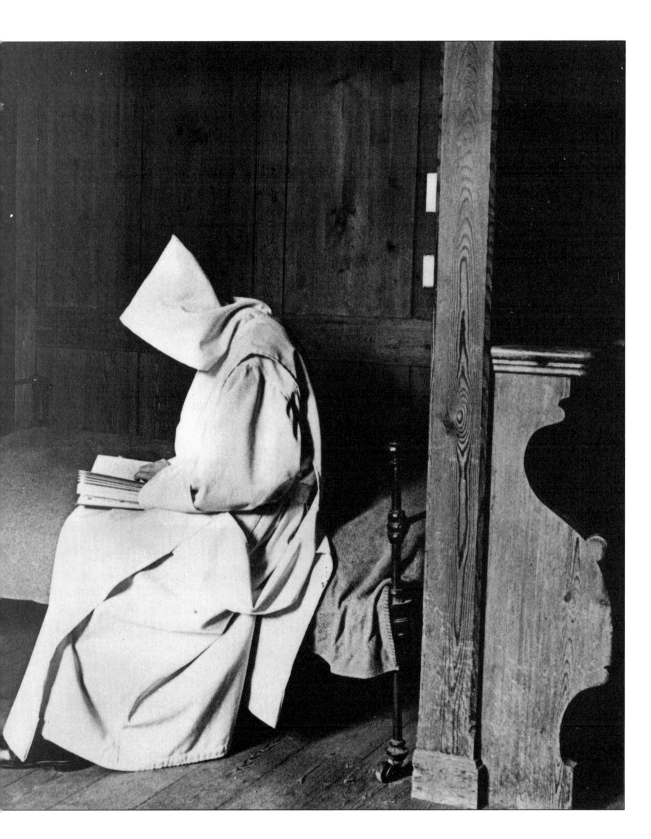

Thereafter, according to the Christian Scriptures, the apostles gained courage and became missionaries, fulfilling the final directive of their risen and ascended Lord: "Go therefore and make disciples of all nations, baptizing them in the name of the Father and of the Son and of the Holy Spirit." (Matt. 28.19) They went about teaching the main Christian message, that Jesus was the Messiah, that he was the Son of God, that he was crucified and raised from the dead, and that through him sins are forgiven and eternal salvation is offered to all people.

Christian historians note that late in his life and ministry, the chief apostle Peter made his way to Rome, the capital city of the Roman Empire, preaching the faith and establishing a Christian community. Paul, a convert from Judaism, also traveled through the Gentile world, and he, too, after "journeying often" arrived at Rome. It was there that both Peter and Paul met their deaths, probably in the same year, A.D. 64, at the orders of the emperor Nero.

This was the beginning of 300 years of persecution for the Christians by the Roman authorities. Christianity was declared illegal, and many Christians died for their faith. Their martyrdom sowed the seeds of faith in the hearts of many converts. After many years of rejection and persecution, Christians began to gain some acceptance. By the time of Constantine (A.D. 280-337), who is considered the first Christian emperor of Rome, the clash between the Christian church and the Roman Empire had begun to lessen. Christianity became the accepted religion of Rome around 380.

This apparent worldly acceptance gradually brought with it a number of problems for Christians. Rome itself was under threat of extinction by the conquering Goths. Some Roman citizens began to raise serious questions about the role of Christians and Christianity in the empire. Could Christians be good citizens that could be depended on to fight for Rome? Or were they so committed to Christ's kingdom that earthly kingdoms and responsibilities had no relevance to them? In short, where do Christians put their loyalty? To which kingdom do they belong?

Questions of this kind were raised because Christianity was not simply the religion of the naive or the simple. In 400 years it had not only attracted the poor and the meek who are so wonderfully portrayed in the Sermon on the Mount; it had also garnered the loyalty of Justin, of Clement of Alexandria, of Irenaeus, of Basil, of Gregory of Nyssa, of Jerome, of Ambrose, of Augustine who were all viewed by later Christians as Fathers of the Church. It had become not only the church of the Sermon on the Mount, but also the church of Irenaeus's learned book *Against the Heretics*, and the church of a forceful work on Christianity and its relation to all worldly concerns, Augustine's *The City of God*. In short, it was a church that had moved into the complicated relationships of government and church, of reason and faith, of worldly success and divine plan. How were these alternatives related to one another? Anyone who reads *The City of God* realizes that it was written by a very wise and prudent Christian wrestling with the very serious problems: How is the Christian community related to the actual societies in which Christians live? Should it condemn them? Should it correct them? Should it compromise with them?

■ *The fish became a symbol of Christ for early Christians, since the Greek word for fish was **ichthus,** which was a summary for **I**esus **Ch**ristos **th**eou **u**ios **s**oter (Jesus Christ, the son of God, Savior).*

From Monte Cassino to the Reformation (529 to 1517)

Rome did fall; but Monte Cassino, the great Benedictine monastery, began. What does this mean? It means that the classical pagan world—with its legal and political accomplishments, artistic achievements, literary education, and philosophical systems—collapsed. The Goths, the barbarians, had won! Yet the culture of the Greco-Roman and early Christian world was preserved and given new life by Cassiodorus and the scribes of Monte Cassino, monks who followed the Rule of Saint Benedict and who gave themselves to the study of the Bible and the classics. Slowly, but surely, the dominant barbarian culture was able to assimilate and blend the various strains of the pagan and Christian cultures of the ancient worlds. Under Charlemagne (800) a great educational reform was headed by the Irish monk Alcuin. Eventually monastic, cathedral, and palace schools developed, where monks and priests and civil clerks and administrators were educated. Out of some of these schools the first universities (Paris, Bologna, Oxford, Montpellier) were born, with their strong faculties of law, medicine, and theology.

Religious Life in the Middle Ages

The monastery of Monte Cassino, founded in 529, was not only a center preserving and fostering classical culture; it was the most famous of a large collection of Benedictine monasteries that breathed new spiritual life into the Christianity of Rome and then spread throughout the Western world. Benedict of Nursia founded a number of monasteries, first at Subiaco, in the mountain region east of Rome, then in a dozen other locations. These were independent ,self-supporting, and self-contained communities of monks, just outside towns or in rural areas, dedicated to prayer, work, and study. The monastic life demands that persons withdraw from worldly affairs to devote themselves completely to religion. A monk's or nun's purpose is to lead a perfect Christian life. Monks and nuns took vows pledging themselves to poverty, chastity, and obedience and spent much of their day in prayer.

After the fall of Rome, in a world of mounting chaos, Benedict's Rule guided these oases of order, decency, justice, and

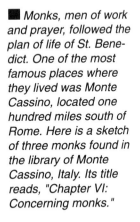 Monks, men of work and prayer, followed the plan of life of St. Benedict. One of the most famous places where they lived was Monte Cassino, located one hundred miles south of Rome. Here is a sketch of three monks found in the library of Monte Cassino, Italy. Its title reads, "Chapter VI: Concerning monks."

spiritual virtue. These religious communities eventually spread far and wide and became centers where the prayer life of the Christian church was fostered, developed, and spread.

The devotion of these abbeys, houses where monks or nuns live, ruled over by abbots (spiritual fathers), centered around the Divine Office. This office consisted of the Book of Psalms, readings from the Old and New Testaments, readings from the early church fathers, and hymns. This book of prayer was structured so that all 150 psalms of the Old Testament were sung each week, with each day divided into eight parts. Every three hours, a part of this Divine Office was chanted. The office sounded a religious rhythm that enveloped the whole day in the spirit of prayer, so that even work and study were done within the atmosphere of prayer. Benedict's Rule was sturdy enough that it by itself, and without any common government, was able to keep order within the many independent monasteries as they multiplied. At times, some laxity and abuses occurred, but even the late 11th and early 12th century reforms of the monasteries of Citeaux and Cluny, which spread to other monasteries, were based essentially on the Rule of Benedict.

Other religious movements gained prominence, especially in the 12th and 13th centuries. As cities began to sprout up throughout Europe, a new kind of ministry was needed besides the one carried on in the monasteries, which were usually separated from urban life. Two of the most influential movements were begun by Saint Francis of Assisi and by Saint Dominic. They founded two religious orders, the Franciscans and the Dominicans, dedicated to poverty and preaching. When the universities began, these orders also became strong participants in the intellectual life there. Among the most famous thinkers of the Middle Ages were Albert the Great and Thomas Aquinas, both Dominicans, Bonaventure, Duns Scotus, and William of Ockham, who were Franciscans. These orders also produced respected preachers such as Raymond of Penafort, Anthony of Padua, Bernardine of Siena, and John Capistran. By their popularity and their influence, these friars inspired the development of similar religious groups, such as the Carmelites and the Hermits of Saint Augustine.

> **■ Founders of Some Religious Orders**
> **St. Benedict**—Benedictines (Roman Catholic)
> **St. Francis**—Franciscans (Roman Catholic)
> **St. Dominic**—Dominicans (Roman Catholic)
> **St. Ignatius Loyola**—Jesuits (Roman Catholic)
> **R. M. Benson**—Cowley Fathers (Anglican)
> **St. Berthold**—Carmelites (Roman Catholic)
> **St. Robert of Molesme**—Trappists (Roman Catholic)
> **Sts. Vincent de Paul and Louise de Marillac**—
>   Sisters of Charity (Roman Catholic)
> **St. John Bosco**—Salesians (Roman Catholic)
> **William J. Butler**—Wantage Community (Anglican)

The Growth of Christianity in the Middle Ages

After the fall of Rome, the church could quite well have fallen into a collection of small feudal churches controlled by local lords. If there was a uniting force that prevented this ecclesiastical splintering, it was the Roman papacy. Especially strong was this force under the papacy of Gregory I, or Gregory the Great, from 590 to 604.

Gregory was the first monk to become pope. In circumstances that were very trying, he fed the poor of Rome; he managed the estates of the church in such a way that while their revenues increased, the cultivators of the land were treated with great humanity. He reformed church music and the celebration of worship within the church and preached fervently and frequently, as can be seen in his "Moral Lessons on the Book of Job." His favorite title, and one that was very appropriate to him, was *servus servorum Dei* ("servant of the servants of God"). In the 9th century, this became the official title for the pope, which shows both Gregory's influence and the high ideals he set for the papacy.

Gregory sent Augustine (of Canterbury) as the head of a small group of missionaries to bring the Christian life and faith to England. A number of Gregory's contemporaries also carried Christianity to other parts of Europe. For example, Columban, an Irish monk, preached to the Franks, and Columcille, by the force

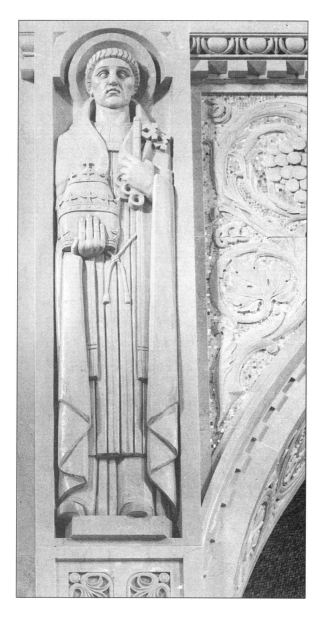

■ *Pope Gregory I, or Gregory the Great, was the first monk to become a pope, or leader of the whole Christian community. He set a high example of papal leadership.*

of his commitment as a monk on the island of Iona, strongly influenced the Christian life of the Scots, Celts, and Picts in Scotland. A century later, Boniface converted the Bavarians, the Thuringians, and all the Germanic peoples. In the latter part of the 10th century, Christianity made rapid headway in Denmark,

Sweden, and Norway. Saint Olaf made the conversion of Norway complete in the 11th century, and even before his death Christianity had spread to the Scandinavian outposts of Greenland and Iceland in the Atlantic and into western Russia.

Although Gregory had set a wonderful example for the papacy, it was not always followed. Still, there are many splendid examples of strong and religious popes in the 11th century: Leo IX (1048-1054), Alexander II (1061-1073), and Gregory VII (1073-1085) are but a few. These reformers, who tried to keep the spiritual power of the papacy free from the control of government rulers and to separate the appointment of bishops from government powers, did not always win their battles. Gregory VII lost to King Henry IV. The 12th century also reveals many strong popes: Innocent II (1130-1143), Eugene III (1145-1153), Alexander III (1159-1181), and Innocent III (1198-1216). They all opposed the dominance of the government rulers of their times and their invasion into the realm of religious authority. "Render unto Caesar the things that are Caesar's, and to God the things that are God's." (Matt. 22.21) Such fights over political and church power became more and more commonplace in the centuries that followed. One famous conflict was between Pope Boniface VIII and Philip the Fair.

The Reformation of 1517 and Its Effects to 1648

The issue of how spiritual and political power interact has many parallels. Does God save man without man's efforts? Or does man merit heaven? Is grace something in man that makes him worthy of eternal life? If so, then it seems that some claim to merit eternal life is essential to humankind. Basically, the issue of spiritual and political power is parallel to the issue of the relationship of the divine and the human, the natural and the supernatural.

Martin Luther, an Augustinian monk, raised these questions in his "Ninety-five Theses," which he nailed to the door of Wittenberg Cathedral on October 31, 1517. He set up a challenge against the Roman Catholic church that contested its compromise with the political regimes and its strong dependence on humankind's works instead of trusting in Christ as humankind's savior. In his pamphlet "On Christian Liberty," he established the division between the political and spiritual, the natural and the supernatural, the human and the divine. According to Luther, the Roman church had compromised too much with this world. It had blurred the distinction between political and religious power with its theory of merit by human efforts and by its doctrine on indulgences, whereby people could claim heavenly rewards in exchange for money. Faith in Jesus Christ alone saves, according to Luther.

The religious world, for him, became more spiritual and less worldly. Luther's basic premise, or proposition, was that religion should always be criticizing too cozy a dependence on worldly things and earthly power. Since there would always be more things to criticize and correct, this protestant premise would lead to more protesting and efforts at improvement, very frequently with separating tendencies. Calvin, Zwingli, Farel, and Bucer all took their turn at protesting and separating from the Roman Church. Even Roman Catholicism began to see reform.

This religious disunity caused political disunity. The religious wars of 1618-1648 were over boundaries between Roman Catholics of the more Latin countries and Protestants of the more northern nations. Many appeals were made in different countries for toleration. This can be seen especially in the work of the philosopher John Locke entitled "On Toleration," written while he was in religious and political exile from his native England.

Growth in the Doctrine of Religious Tolerance (1648 to 1815)

As the tensions between Roman Catholicism and Protestantism continued, efforts were made to formalize the appeal of Locke for toleration. In "The Social Contract," for instance, the French philosopher Jean-Jacques Rousseau attempted to lessen religious friction by declaring that certain broader tenets of religion had to be agreed on in a society if it were to avoid self-destruction. These would be religious principles that all had to accept. Rousseau listed some possibilities—that there is a God who knows all things, that he punishes the wicked and rewards the good, that he is offended when we do not keep our agreements or contracts. He goes on to explain that in other matters of

■ *Religious processions, celebrating the feasts of the church, are part of religious life in many Christian countries. Candles not only light the evening march; they symbolize Jesus Christ as the "light of the world."*

religion—those based on private, personal feelings and about which there is no agreement—people must be tolerant.

The Nature of Christianity in the 19th and 20th Centuries

Despite many anti-Christian forces at work in Europe in the 18th and 19th centuries, Christianity spread from Europe to many nations. Before the 19th century this had been due mostly to the greatness of Spain and Portugal, with the result that Roman Catholicism was the form of Christianity that was carried to South and Central America, to the Louisiana Territory, eastern

Canada, and the southwestern United States. In the 19th century, England came into its own and became a strong influence in carrying Anglicanism and many forms of Protestantism to Canada, the United States, Australia, and New Zealand. With the wave of immigrants from Ireland, Italy, southern Germany, Poland, Portugal, and Spain, Roman Catholicism began to have strong influence once again in North America. The vitality of Christianity in its many forms was quite evident in the 19th century.

American Christianity, both Roman Catholic and Protestant, had a very distinctive character. Roman Catholicism was socially active, due to the large number of poor immigrants who needed assistance in getting food, housing, and work. Protestantism, in 19th-century America, also saw the need to help the many poor, needy, and unsettled. With some awareness that anti-Christian forces in Europe charged Christianity with being "other-worldly," Protestant leaders aimed at the transformation of society and had the goal of bringing American society in complete accord with Christian standards. Protestant social activism was responsible for many of the basic and compelling ideals of America. It pushed strongly for the ending of slavery and then for education that might bring economic equality. It also fought the excessive use of alcoholic beverages and demanded better care of the sick, the orphaned, the blind, and the poor. Numerous Christian social organizations have made their impact on the betterment of American society and continue to be a positive force today. Both Catholic and Protestant churches were marked by this activism.

CHAPTER **4**

Branches of Christianity and Their Basic Beliefs

From its beginnings as a sect of Judaism, Christianity has undergone many changes over the course of history. The single church of ancient times divided again and again, evolving from one Christian church into many Christian churches, each with its own beliefs and practices.

The first major division within Christianity was that between the Eastern and Western churches, which occurred in 1054. (The Eastern churches are the major Christian churches in Greece, Russia, eastern Europe, and western Asia). These churches had been drifting apart for centuries, but the ultimate cause of the split was a dispute that began in the 800s. The main issue of the dispute was the Roman pope's claim to authority over the Eastern church. In 1054, delegates of Pope Leo IX excommunicated the patriarch of Constantinople, Michael Cerularius. In turn, the patriarch summoned a council that excommunicated the papal delegates! (To excommunicate someone is to cut that person off from membership in the church.) Attempts to reconcile the two churches in 1274 and 1439 failed. Since 1054 there have been two Christian churches, the Roman Catholic church in the West and the Eastern Orthodox church in the East.

During the 16th century, the Reformation, which was a reform movement within Catholicism, led to a further split and the development of Protestantism. The term Protestant first came into use in 1529 when several princes and leaders of 14 German cities protested an attempt by the Roman Catholic emperor Charles V to end the practice of Lutheranism, an early Protestant movement, and restore Catholic doctrine and worship throughout the Holy Roman Empire. The princes and cities came to be known as the "Protesting Estates." The term Protestant thereafter came to include all Christians of continental Europe who left the Roman Catholic church or were members of a community that descended from a church separated from Rome.

While Martin Luther's ideas were dividing Europe into the Protestant north and the Catholic south, King Henry VIII of England entered into a dispute with Pope Clement VII. Henry, wishing to end his marriage to Catherine of Aragon and to wed Anne Boleyn, sought a papal annulment of his marriage. When Pope Clement refused to grant the annulment, Henry took matters into his own hands. He had himself named supreme head of the Church in England and required all clergymen to swear allegiance to himself instead of to the pope. This was the beginning of the Anglican Church.

Thus, by the middle of the 16th century, Christianity had divided into the four main branches that are recognized today: Roman Catholicism, Eastern Orthodoxy, Protestantism, and Anglicanism.

Roman Catholicism and Its Beliefs

The Incarnation—the belief that God became man by the union of his divine and human natures in the person of Jesus Christ—is the mystery that lies at the heart of all Catholic belief. Old Testament prophecies anticipated this event, and the New Testament bears witness to its reality.

Catholics believe that there is only one God. But in this God there are three persons: the Father, the Son (who became man in Christ), and the Holy Spirit. This mystery, the Holy Trinity, was revealed through the Incarnation and Christ's teachings. Catholic tradition considers God the Father as neither created nor begotten (coming forth from another person), the Son as begotten of (coming forth from) God the Father, and the Holy Spirit as proceeding from both the Father and the Son as the bond of the divine love that unites them.

The Athanasian Creed (written between 434 and 440) sums up the fundamental theological beliefs of the Catholic church:

And the Catholic Faith is this: we worship one God in Trinity, and Trinity in Unity, neither confounding the Persons, nor dividing the Substance. For there is one person of the Father, another of the Son, another of the Holy Ghost. But the Godhead of the Father, of the Son, and of the Holy Ghost is all one: the Glory co-equal, the Majesty co-eternal.

And in this Trinity none is before or after the other; none is the greater or less than another; but the whole three Persons are co-eternal together, and co-equal; so that in all things the Unity in Trinity, and the Trinity in Unity is to be worshipped. He therefore that will be saved must thus think of the Trinity.

Furthermore, it is necessary to everlasting salvation that he also believe rightly in the Incarnation of our Lord Jesus Christ. For the right Faith is, that we believe and confess, that our Lord Jesus Christ, the Son of God, is God and Man. . . . He suffered for our salvation, descended into hell, rose again the third day from the dead. He ascended into heaven, sitteth at the right hand of the Father, God Almighty, from whence He shall come to judge the living and the dead. At his coming all men shall rise again with their bodies and shall give account for their own works. They that have done good shall go to life everlasting, and they that have done evil into everlasting fire.

This is the Catholic Faith. Unless a man believe it faithfully, he cannot be saved.

The Catholic church teaches that humankind's destiny, set by God, is to share God's life for eternity. However, the original sin—the disobedience to God's commands by the first man, Adam—interfered with God's plan. Adam's original sin passes to each child born in the world and is manifest in each person's innate inclination to disobey God's commands. To save human-kind from all sin, both the inherited original sin and actual sins committed during a person's lifetime due to our inclination to evil, God sent his Son to earth. Through his life, death, and resurrection, Jesus reopened for humanity the possibility of at-taining its original spiritual destiny. Through his teachings and his church, Christ teaches people the way to realize this destiny. Salvation will be given to all who believe in the Holy Trinity and are sincerely sorry for their sins.

According to Catholic doctrine, life does not end with the death of the body. Instead, the soul leaves the body and goes to one of three places: heaven, purgatory, or hell. Heaven is the community of those who made amends for their forgiven sins and who have been united with God. Purgatory is a temporary state for those who must be purified of imperfection or make amends for sins already forgiven. Hell is the endless absence of God, the punishment for persons who have rejected God through the enormity of their unforgiven sins.

Another important part of Catholic faith is the veneration or special honor given to Mary, the mother of Christ. She is also called the Blessed Virgin. The special nature of her motherhood is told in the Gospel of Luke (1:26-38):

> *And in the sixth month the angel Gabriel was sent from God unto a city of Galilee, named Nazareth, to a virgin espoused to a man whose name was Joseph, of the house of David; and the virgin's name was Mary.*
>
> *And the angel came in unto her, and said, "Hail, thou that art highly favored, the Lord is with thee: blessed art thou among women."*
>
> *And when she saw him, she was troubled at his saying, and cast in her mind what manner of salutation this should be.*
>
> *And the angel said unto her, "Fear not, Mary: for thou hast found favor with God. And behold, thou shalt*

conceive in thy womb, and bring forth a son, and shalt call his name JESUS. He shall be great, and shall be called the Son of the Highest: and the Lord God shall give unto him the throne of his father David: And he shall reign over the house of Jacob for ever; and of his kingdom there shall be no end."

Then said Mary unto the angel, "How shall this be, seeing I know not a man?"

And the angel answered and said unto her, "The Holy Spirit shall come upon thee, and the power of the Highest shall overshadow thee: therefore also that holy thing which shall be born of thee shall be called the Son of God. . . .For with God nothing shall be impossible."

And Mary said, "Behold the handmaid of the Lord; be it done unto me according to thy word." And the angel departed from her.

There is great significance in Mary's role as the mother of Jesus. When she became the mother of Jesus, she also became the mother of the church itself that descended from him.

Catholics also honor a great number of saints. Saints are persons who have led exceptionally holy lives and who have been formally recognized by the church as having attained an exalted position in heaven and as being entitled to veneration on earth. The Virgin Mary is recognized as a saint, as are the apostles and many early Christian martyrs. Statues of Mary and of the saints have prominent places in Roman Catholic churches and are honored as symbols of the holy people they represent.

The beliefs of Roman Catholics are based on both the Bible and church traditions. These traditions have come from a number of sources: the declarations of church councils and popes, the teachings of the ancient fathers of the church, and short statements of belief called creeds, such as the Apostles' Creed, the Athanasian Creed, and the Nicene Creed.

Worship and Liturgy

The public acts of worship that Catholics perform together are called the liturgy. The central act of liturgy is the Eucharist, or

> ■ **Prayer to Mary: The Hail Mary (Ave Maria)**
>
> *Hail Mary, full of Grace. The Lord is with thee. Blessed art thou amongst women, and blessed is the fruit of thy womb, Jesus. Holy Mary, Mother of God, pray for us sinners now and at the hour of our death. Amen.*

Mass. Weekly attendance at Mass and attendance on holy days of obligation, such as Christmas, are required of all church members. Other important liturgical acts include the seven sacraments, one of which is Holy Eucharist. In addition, Catholics carry out acts of devotion to Mary and the saints, such as novenas—devotions consisting of prayers or services held on nine consecutive days or weeks. Sacramentals also play an important part in Catholic piety. They are holy objects or actions that the church has set apart for use as a help toward salvation. Sacramental objects include the crucifix, holy pictures, and statues. Sacramental actions include the blessing of homes, harvests, fishing boats, and animals.

The Mass has two main parts, the liturgy of the word and the Eucharistic liturgy. The liturgy of the word consists of a petition for forgiveness of sins, hymns, prayers, biblical readings, a homily or sermon concerning these readings, and a declaration of faith. The Eucharistic liturgy is a celebration of the Lord's Supper, also known as the Last Supper—the meal Jesus shared with his disciples the evening before his crucifixion. Gifts of bread and wine are offered to God. The priest, acting in Jesus' name and with his power, according to Catholic faith, changes these gifts into Christ's body and blood. The congregation then receives, under the appearance of bread and wine, the body and blood of Christ. The Catholic church teaches firmly that the Eucharist involves an actual change: in faith the Catholic accepts that the sacrament is not just a symbol of Christ's body and blood; it is the body and blood of Christ.

For a long time the Mass, or Eucharist, was celebrated only in Latin, the official language of the church over the centuries. To allow greater participation by the congregation, the Constitution on the Sacred Liturgy approved by Vatican II, a worldwide church council held from 1962 to 1965, permitted the use of the vernacular (the local language) in place of Latin. The vernacular was also approved for the celebration of other sacraments.

The seven sacraments of the Catholic church are ceremonial signs of God's action in people's lives. Catholics believe that the sacraments are the sources, or means, by which a person attains a state of grace—the condition of being in God's favor. According to Catholic faith, three elements are involved in sacraments: the outward, or sensible, signs (the substances used, such as water, oil, bread and wine), the form (the words pronounced by the priest), and the power (to effect the sacraments granted to the church by Christ), whereby the sensible substances signify spiritual realities and also cause such spiritual realities to occur. A detailed discussion of the seven sacraments follows.

Baptism is the ceremony in which a child, or an adult convert, is cleansed of sin to begin a new life with God. In the name of the Trinity, water is poured over the head of the person being baptized as a sign both that the person is being cleansed of sin and that a new spiritual life is flowing into the baptized. Baptism also marks the beginning of a Catholic's joining in oneness with Christ, entry into the community of the church and God's granting to the baptized the fundamental condition necessary for heaven or for union with the saints or blessed in heaven.

Confirmation strengthens a baptized person in the Christian faith and confers the grace that will enable that person to grow to spiritual adulthood. It is the spiritual coming-of-age of the Catholic. During this ceremony, a bishop marks the sign of the cross in chrism, or holy oil (a sign of strength), on the forehead of the person being confirmed.

The Eucharist, or Mass, is the central act of the Catholics' worship of God and is described above.

Reconciliation, also called penance or confession, is a sacrament in which Catholics confess their sins to a priest, express their sincere sorrow for having sinned, promise not to sin in the future, and voice a willingness to make satisfaction for the sins. The priest forgives the sinner with the statement "I absolve thee from thy sins in the name of the Father and of the Son and of the Holy Spirit." At the end of the confession, the priest assigns a penance to the penitent, which that person is to perform in satisfaction for his or her sins.

Matrimony is the sacrament in which a man and a woman bind themselves to each other as husband and wife for life. Their Christian marriage is meant to illustrate or be a symbol of Christ's marriage to his church. Catholic teaching does not recognize divorce or allow divorced persons to remarry, unless the original "marriage" has been annulled—declared by church law to have been invalid.

Holy orders is the sacrament in which men chosen by the church are made deacons, priests, or bishops. The principal powers of the priesthood are those Christ gave his apostles, who were the first priests: to offer Mass, forgive sins, administer the sacraments, and preach the gospel. The priests of the early church were often married, but rules regarding the celibacy of the priesthood became increasingly widespread, and by the Lateran Council of 1123, celibacy became the rule for all clergy and even up to the present day, Catholic priests are not permitted to be married.

Last anointing, or extreme unction, is a sacrament given to persons who are seriously ill or in danger of death from illness or accident. The priest anoints the person's sense organs with oil, saying, "By this holy unction and His most tender mercy, may the Lord pardon thee whatever sin thou hast committed by thy sight, by thy hearing. . . ." Last anointing forgives all sins for which the person is truly sorry. It confers grace and prepares the soul for death.

Church Organization

The hierarchy of the Catholic church has three levels: the pope, who is the bishop of Rome and the spiritual leader of the worldwide church; bishops, who are responsible for a diocese, or territorial district; and pastors, who are spiritual leaders of individual parishes. The pope appoints the bishops, who in turn appoint pastors.

Assisting the pope in governing the church are two bodies, the college of cardinals and the Roman curia. The college of cardinals is a group of Catholics, most often clergymen, appointed by the pope to serve as his advisers. They have the responsibility of electing a new pope when necessary. The Roman curia serves as the pope's administrative arm. It consists of the secretariat of state, which assists the pope most directly in both governing the church and communicating with the rest of the curia, and a number of other departments, each of which has a specific function.

Roman Catholics believe that the pope is infallible in matters of faith and morals. This means that when the pope speaks *ex cathedra*, or by virtue of his office, he cannot commit a doctrinal error. The pope does not have infallibility in connection with other aspects of church affairs, but he does have absolute authority. He is considered the highest teacher, judge, and governing power of the church.

The pope is the ruler of Vatican City, an independent state within the city of Rome, Italy. The Vatican has its own flag, coins, stamps, and public works. As an independent state, it has diplomatic status, and the pope sends representatives to other countries and receives ambassadors from them.

The strict governing power of the church over its members is twofold. It has a legislative, or lawmaking, role and a judicial role pertaining to the administration of church law. Church laws regulate the conduct of the church and its members. Church courts make decisions in matters pertaining to church law and apply penalties when called for or excuse from violations in cases where no law was broken. The ultimate penalty is excommunication, which declares a person cut off from the life of the church and from the reception of the sacraments. The chief role of the church, however, is not to judge, but to teach and exhort through its teaching. It is in few cases that the church deals with its members through any official legal system; generally it instructs through teaching and exhortation.

Observances

In the early years of Christianity, many Christians assumed that the Second Coming of Christ was near and that the world would soon come to an end. Up until the fourth century, the church formally celebrated only Sundays, Easter, and Pentecost, holy days related to the redemption of humankind. As Christians began to accept that the world had not come to an end and was unlikely to come to an end any time soon, they also accepted as a reminder of ideal Christian life on earth a calendar of feast days that had been developing informally. By the Middle Ages, each day of the year honored a saint, an event, or a religious reality, such as the Trinity.

Christian holy days often transformed traditional pagan festivals. For example, ceremonies and symbols associated with the vernal equinox—the beginning of spring—took on new depth and meaning and came to represent Christ's resurrection. December 25 was celebrated in pagan Rome as the feast of Sol Invictus, the unconquered sun. Kindling of the Yule log, decorating houses with holly and evergreens, and adorning an evergreen tree were magical pagan acts to encourage the sun's return. For Christians, Christ is the light of the world, the spiritual Sun. Christians gave the pagan feasts a new meaning, and many pagan symbols were converted to express different facets of the new Christian meaning.

The Catholic year is still marked by the observance of a multitude of feasts and festivals, the most important of which commemorate major events in the life of Jesus Christ. Some festivals, however, are called particular feasts, in contrast to the feasts of the calendar of the universal church. These particular feasts are celebrated only in certain parts of the world. For example, a town may hold a festival for its patron saint. Among the most important universal church observances are these:

- **Feast of Mary**, Mother of God (January 1)
- **Lent** (period beginning forty weekdays before Easter): an annual season of fasting and penitence in preparation for Easter
- **Palm Sunday** (Sunday before Easter): commemorates Christ's triumphal entry into Jerusalem
- **Holy Thursday** (Thursday before Easter): celebrates Jesus' gift of his body and blood in the Eucharist; the anniversary of the Last Supper
- **Good Friday** (Friday before Easter): the anniversary of the crucifixion of Christ
- **Easter** (first Sunday after the first full moon following the vernal equinox): celebrates the resurrection of Jesus
- **Ascension Day** (fortieth day after Easter): celebrates the ascension, or rising, of Christ to heaven
- **Pentecost** (seventh Sunday after Easter): commemorates the descent of the Holy Spirit on the disciples
- **Assumption of Mary** (August 15): celebrates the day on which God assumed the body of Mary into heaven
- **All Saints' Day** (November 1): celebrates all the saints

- **All Souls' Day** (November 2): a day of solemn prayer in memory of all the dead who have not yet attained heaven
- **Immaculate Conception** (December 8): celebrates the sinlessness of Mary, the mother of Christ
- **Christmas** (December 25): celebrates the birth of Christ

Eastern Orthodoxy and Its Beliefs

To Orthodox Christians, God is both unknown and yet well known. God cannot be described in words but only understood in a union of love. The essence of God—his true nature—is a mystery beyond human understanding. The divine energies, God's actions among people, express his nearness and are the only ways in which humans can know God.

Like Roman Catholics, Orthodox Christians believe that God is a Trinity of Father, Son, and Holy Spirit and that human beings are created in the image of God. This means that human beings are also formed in the image of the Trinity—a triad of divine persons united in love. Human beings, therefore, are not meant to live in isolation, unloving and unloved. Humans are created for relationship and sharing. It is the task of humans to create, both in the church and in society, the movement of mutual love that exists within God the Trinity. To the Orthodox church, the Son of God, Jesus Christ, became fully human, having not only a human body but a human soul, human impulses, and human feelings. Yet at the same time, he is still God. Orthodoxy accepts as literally true the statements in the Bible about the virgin birth, Christ's miracles, and the resurrection. Christ destroyed the ultimate power of evil by his death on the cross and his resurrection. To Orthodox Christians, Christ is a victorious king, not in spite of the crucifixion but because of it. His resurrection conquered bodily death and made Christ ruler of a new kingdom.

Orthodoxy looks upon the Holy Spirit not just as a manifestation of God's presence among people but as an equal member of the Trinity. The church, guided by the Holy Spirit, is the realization of the Kingdom of God on earth.

Eastern Orthodox churches teach that their church is faithful to the teachings of the apostles and free from errors in matters of doctrine. One of the differences in the doctrines of the Eastern

Top-Cross of the Crusades, which became known as the Jerusalem cross.
Middle-The Chi(X) Rho(P) cross carries in it the first letters-**Ch** and **r**-in the name of **Chr**ist.
Bottom-The Celtic cross includes the circle of the sun which reminds those who look at it that the Christ who died on the cross is the Light or Sun of the spiritual world.

Orthodox churches and the Roman Catholic church is in the text of the Nicene Creed, a statement of Christian faith adopted at the Council of Nicaea in 325. Orthodox Christians use the original text, which states that the Holy Spirit proceeds from the Father. Roman Catholics and other Western Christians use a later form of the text that states that the Holy Spirit proceeds from the Father and from the Son.

One of the unique features of Orthodox Christianity is the importance of icons, representations in paint or enamel of sacred personages, such as Christ or the saints. The icons themselves are venerated and considered sacred. The Orthodox doctrine of icons grows out of the belief that all of God's creation, material and spiritual, is to be redeemed and glorified. Icons are not just paintings, they are instruments of grace.

A long dispute over the presence in churches of images of Christ and the saints came to a head in the year 726, when Emperor Leo III issued an order that all images and paintings in churches be covered or destroyed. This decree served to divide the church into two groups: iconoclasts, who favored removing the images from the churches, and monks and the people in general, who opposed the iconoclasts. After the second Nicene Council in 787, the empress Irene permitted worship of images as long as this worship had a different quality than that owed to God. In 843, the use of icons in churches was fully restored, so long as these were confined to pictures. Sculpted figures were no longer used.

Worship and Liturgy

Services in the Eastern Orthodox churches consist of the Divine Liturgy, the Divine Office, and Occasional Offices. Daily church services are based on the Bible, especially on the Psalms, and include hymns and prayers that comment on biblical events. All services are sung or chanted, usually in the language of the congregation.

The Divine Liturgy is the celebration of the Eucharist. Although some of the liturgy, which recalls Christ's entire life, is enacted by the priests, the Orthodox congregation feels itself to be taking part in the service. The images of Christ and the saints depicted around the church show that they too are present.

The Divine Office consists of prayers and readings called matins and vespers and several lesser offices. Occasional Offices include services for baptism or marriage.

Eastern Orthodox churches have the same seven major sacraments as the Roman Catholic church described earlier. There are, however, some important differences between the celebration of the sacraments in the two churches.

Baptism admits infants and adult converts into the church, as in Roman Catholicism. In carrying out the baptism, however, the priest dips the body of the person being baptized into water three times, saying, "The servant of God is baptized in the name of the Father and of the Son and of the Holy Spirit."

Chrismation, or confirmation, is administered immediately after baptism. This grants the newly baptized person full membership in the church and the right to participate in the Eucharist. The forehead and other parts of the body of the person being confirmed are anointed with holy oil, or chrism, with the words "the seal of the gift of the Holy Spirit."

The Eucharist is the part of the Eastern Orthodox service called the Divine Liturgy. It recalls Christ's life and includes the taking of Holy Communion as a way of helping the worshipers realize the presence of the risen Christ in them and his victory over death. As in Roman Catholicism, it is believed that the bread and wine consecrated in the Eucharist become the true body and blood of Christ. At every Eucharist, Christ himself is seen to be the true celebrant, both priest who offers the sacrament and victim whose body and blood are being offered. All major church rituals are centered around the Eucharist.

Confession, or penance, is a sacrament in which a person confesses sins to God in the presence of a priest. The priest forgives the sins in the name of God and offers the person spiritual advice.

Matrimony joins a man and a woman together and forms a family. Unlike the Roman Catholic church, Eastern Orthodox churches permit divorce and allow divorced persons to remarry, but the first marriage is considered the greatest in the eyes of God. Most Orthodox churches permit only three marriages.

Holy orders admit men to the major (bishops, priests, and deacons) and minor (subdeacons and readers) orders of the clergy.

The Eastern Orthodox churches are the major Christian churches in Greece, Russia, eastern Europe, and western Asia. Archbishop Iakavos is the leader of the Greek Orthodox church of North and South America.

Here again there is a difference with the Roman Catholic church, since the Orthodox priesthood includes both married and monastic clergy. Married clergy head parishes, and monastic clergy usually live in monasteries. Priests and deacons cannot marry after they are ordained, however, and only unmarried priests can become bishops.

Anointing of the sick is a sacrament in which a priest anoints a sick person and prays for forgiveness of the person's sins and for his or her recovery. This sacrament is not restricted to those who are near death and can be conferred on any who ask for it.

Church Organization

As we have said, the Eastern Orthodox churches are the major Christian churches in Greece, Russia, eastern Europe, and western Asia. Individually, they are usually called by their national names, such as the Greek Orthodox church or the Russian Orthodox church, but they are united by common beliefs and traditions. Some churches are independent and self-governing; others, primarily churches that were established by missionaries, are not self-governing. The self-governing churches of Constantinople, Alexandria, Antioch, and Jerusalem hold places of special honor for historical reasons. The greatest honor is given to the leader of the Church of Constantinople, who is called the ecumenical patriarch. Although honored, he has authority only over his own church.

The three major orders of Orthodox clergy are the bishops, priests, and deacons; the two minor orders are the subdeacons and readers. Deacons, subdeacons, and readers assist the priest during religious services. Both the spiritual life and the administration of the churches are governed by the principle of shared responsibility between the clergy and the laity, or nonclergy. The laity often take part in the administration of their church and in the election of their clergy.

Observances

As with Roman Catholicism, the most important festivals of Eastern Orthodoxy commemorate major events in the life of Christ, such as Christmas, Palm Sunday, Holy (Good) Friday, Easter, and Pentecost. East and West, though, celebrate many feasts differently. For example, January 6, honored in Egypt as the birthday of Osiris and celebrated as a pagan water festival, became renowned in the East as the date of Christ's baptism. In the Roman Catholic church, this same date commemorates the adoration of the Magi, the three wise men who came to worship Christ when he was born. The climax of the Eastern church's year is Easter.

Some Orthodox churches' holy days are celebrated on different dates than in other branches of Christianity. This is because these churches use the old, or Julian, calendar, which is 13 days behind the new, or Gregorian, calendar in common use throughout the world. According to the Gregorian calendar, special Orthodox holy days are as follows:

- **Baptism of Jesus** (January 6)
- **Sunday of Orthodoxy** (first Sunday of Lent): a solemn festival held to commemorate the restoration of the use of icons in the church (A.D. 843) and the triumph over all heresies
- **Annunciation** (March 25): the announcement by the angel Gabriel to the Virgin Mary of the Incarnation of Christ
- **Saints Peter and Paul** (June 29): celebrates the martyrdom of the chief apostles of the Christian church
- **The Feast of the Holy Apostles** (June 30)
- **Transfiguration of Jesus Christ** (August 6): celebrates the supernatural and glorified change in the appearance of Jesus on the mountain described in the Gospel of Matthew (17:1-9)
- **Falling Asleep** (Death) **of the Most Holy Mother of God** (August 15)
- **The Elevation of the Holy Cross** (September 14): commemorates the finding of the Holy Cross by Saint Helen and its recovery after it had been stolen in the seventh century
- **The Nativity of Jesus Christ** (December 25): Christmas Day

Protestantism and Its Beliefs

Protestantism, which arose in the Reformation movement of the 16th century, is the youngest branch of Christianity. It actually developed as a series of semi-independent religious movements, each of which rejected the central authority of the pope, rather than as one movement. Cultural, geographic, and political differences caused these movements to develop independently in various degrees. Compared with the unity that characterizes the Roman Catholic church and the Eastern Orthodox church, which date from the earliest days of the Christian era, Protestantism has itself divided into hundreds of separate denominations and sects. Some of these deny all relationship to the others! Each of the many denominations has differing beliefs and practices; thus they appear to be entirely distinct from one another. It is difficult, therefore, to discuss Protestantism as a single branch of Christianity.

Protestants as a whole share a belief in one God and in the central importance of Jesus Christ as the savior of humanity. Many denominations also believe in the Trinity of Father, Son, and Holy Spirit.

Protestants differ with other Christians about the fundamental relationship between humanity and God. Protestants oppose the Roman Catholic doctrine on salvation, which teaches that people achieve salvation by having faith in God's grace and by their own efforts performed while in the state of God's grace—doing good works. Protestantism rests on the belief that God deals directly with the individual, so that salvation is gained by faith alone in Christ's redemption. Good works should express

■ The Mormon Temple is the mother church of the Church of Jesus Christ of Latter Day Saints in Salt Lake City, Utah. The Tabernacle at the left houses a huge organ and a 375-member choir.

our gratitude for Christ's redeeming death, but they play no part in meriting salvation. This idea was first put forth by Martin Luther:

> *Therefore the first care of every Christian ought to be, to lay aside all reliance on works, and strengthen his faith alone more and more, and by it grow in the knowledge, not of works, but of Christ Jesus, who has suffered and risen again for him; as Peter teaches, when he makes no other work to be a Christian one. Thus Christ, when the Jews asked Him what they should do that they might work the works of God, rejected the multitude of works, with which He saw that they were puffed up, and commanded them one thing only, saying: "This is the work of God, that ye believe in him whom He hath sent, for him hath God the Father sealed"*
> *(John 6.27, 29)*

Whereas the beliefs of Roman Catholics are based on both the Bible and church traditions, most Protestants believe that the Bible should be the only authority for their religion. The Helvetic Confession, written by Henry Bullinger (1504-1575), set out beliefs that are widely used in Reformed churches:

> *We believe and confess that the Canonical Scriptures of the Old and New Testaments are the true Word of God, and have sufficient authority in and of themselves, and not from men: since God himself through them still speaks to us, as He did to the Fathers, the Prophets, and Apostles. They contain all that is necessary to a saving faith and a holy life; and hence nothing could be added to or taken from them.*

Although there are central beliefs shared by most Protestants, there are also many important differences among them. These divergent views have resulted in the division of Protestantism into different religious groups or sects.

The Early Protestant Churches

Even though the number of Protestant churches are legion and it is impossible to describe all the different views of Christian life that they represent, there are the early or root churches that set up many of the basic principles for the many new religious communities that descend from them.

1. The Lutherans

Martin Luther (1483-1546), after university studies at Erfurt, Germany, entered a cloister of Augustinian hermits and was ordained a priest in 1507. He received his doctorate in Theology at the University of Wittenberg in 1512 and began a teaching career there that lasted all his life. He became deeply involved in the controversy over indulgences (a practice that allowed the papal remission of the temporal punishment due to sin). Abuses flowing from this practice often justified the offering of indulgences by the pope or those claiming papal approval as a means of raising money. Luther saw this practice as indicative of the way in which the Catholic Church had compromised the spiritual mission of Christianity and become too worldly in its interests. Mainly through this controversy, he arrived at the conclusion that the fundamental difficulties between the Catholic and his new interpretation of Christianity were too great. He accentuated the differences in his theology and his theological positions led to his excommunication by Pope Leo X, a condemnation that was carried out in 1521 by the Emperor Charles at the Diet of Worms (a meeting of princes, nobles and clergymen). At this meeting Luther, when asked to retract his teachings declared:

> *Unless I am convinced by the testimony of the Scriptures or by clear reason (for I do not trust either in the pope or councils alone, since it is well known that they have often erred and contradicted themselves), I am bound by the Scriptures I have quoted and my conscience is captive to the Word of God. I cannot and I will not retract anything, since it is neither safe nor right to go against conscience. I cannot do otherwise.*

In his *Babylonian Captivity of the Church*, Luther attacked the mechanical sacramental rituals of the Catholic Church and in *On Christian Liberty* he glorified the freedom of the Gospel and the importance of personal faith in contrast to what he considered the slavery of Catholics to a worldly ecclesiastical system.

Martin Luther, the father of the Lutheran church, called for dramatic reform within the Christian church and strongly criticized the worldly compromises of the Catholic church.

The chief theologian among Luther's followers was Philip Melanchton, who drew up the Augsburg Confession that enunciates the basic principles of Lutheran faith. Lutherans retained the Mass but eliminated its significance as a sacrifice. German replaced Latin in the service; and the people were given the right to choose their own pastors. In the worship service the sermon assumed the principal place, for the stimulus of the spoken word was imperative to increase personal faith. Some of the Catholic feasts were discarded, although Christmas, Easter and other central festivals were retained.

Lutheranism spread to Denmark, Norway, and Sweden, mainly through students who had studied under Lutheran professors in Germany. It is from these Teutonic nations that Lutheranism spread to North America and other parts of the globe. In the United States many different groups of Lutherans (for example, the American Evangelical Lutheran Church, the Augustana Evangelical Lutheran Church, The Finnish Evangelican Lutheran Church, and the United Lutheran Church in America) formed the Lutheran Church in America in 1962. This group merged with the American Lutheran Church and the Association of Evangelical Lutheran Churches in 1982. So, in effect, in the United States there are two great Lutheran synods or congregations: the ever-merging one we have just described and the Lutheran Church—Missouri Synod.

2. The Anabaptists of Switzerland

Ulrich Zwingli (1484-1531) also was a reformer. Like Luther he saw abuses in the system of indulgences; but his critique of the Catholic Church was even more radical than that of Luther. He accepted the Bible as the supreme authority in religion and his zeal led him to ban processions, festivals, feasts, confessions and penances, and even the organ in Church. In brief, he was ready to do away with everything the Bible did not support. In 1529, Zwingli met with Luther in Marburg, Germany, to discuss their differing interpretations of the Eucharist, but came to no agreement. For Luther, Christ is really present in the Eucharist, since he gave a literal interpretation to Christ's words: "This is My body." For Zwingli, the Eucharist is a sacrament of thanksgiving to God for the grace He has given through the Gospel. The bread and wine are mere symbols of Christ's body and blood. This debate caused the first major split in Protestantism.

Zwingli's followers were called Anabaptists because they rebaptized those who joined their community, and they refused baptism to infants because they judged them not old enough to have a personal commitment of faith. For Zwingli and his followers, personal faith and religion is essential to Christian life. The Anabaptists were opposed both by the Catholics and the Lutherans, and died out in Germany. They did, however, become numerous in Switzerland and the Austrian Tyrol. In Holland they persisted as Mennonites, taking their name from their leader Menno Simons. The Mennonites have had strong communities in parts of the United States, for example, in the early Germantown before it became part of Philadelphia, in Lancaster, Pennsylvania, and many other rural areas of New York, Pennsylvania, and California where the simple life and personal religious commitment could flourish.

The term "Anabaptists" meant "rebaptizers", and signified those who distrusted the validity of child baptisms. "Baptists" is a shortened form, and its coinage was gradual. The progression, at least in 17th century New England, ran along the following lines: from "The Church of Christ" to "The Church of Christ in the Gospel Order," to "Church of Christ Baptized Upon Profession of Their Faith" to " The Baptized Church of Christ" to the "Baptist Church." The Mennonites, as indicated, are closer to the original "Anabaptists" than 20th-century English or American "Baptists," who owe their descent more to Puritan criticisms of an Anglican Church whose episcopal order, for them, resembled too distinctly the Church of Rome. The Puritans wanted a church that was a voluntary society, not one into which you were born, that is, they wanted their members to choose to belong, as they did at adult Baptism.

"Baptists" arose in England in the early 1600s under the leadership of Thomas Helwys, John Smyth, and John Murton, but became particularly strong in the 1630s under the Calvinist influence of John Spilsbury. One of the members of his group, Mark Lucar, brought the "new baptism" to New England. The Baptists grew in strength during the 18th century when the Great Awakening made traveling evangelism popular and pervasive. After the American Revolution, Baptists made impressive advances among the nation's blacks. English and American Baptists account for nearly 90% of all Baptists worldwide.

3. The Calvinists

John Calvin (1509-1564), though born a Roman Catholic in France, declared himself a Protestant in 1533 and settled in Basel, Switzerland a year later. There he produced in 1536 his *Institutes of the Christian Religion*. This Protestant textbook of theology, written at the age of 26, made him the recognized spokesman for

■ The Plains, Georgia Baptist Church is the parish of former president of the United States, Jimmy Carter.

Christian reform in France and Switzerland. In the same year he was asked to become the leader of Geneva's circle of Protestant pastors. They declared the church superior to the State and demanded the assistance of the State in their attempts to purify church members by strict discipline. This effort earned them banishment at first; but in 1541 the Geneva city council begged Calvin to return and provide able religious and political leadership.

Although he believed that organization could make it easier to enforce purer discipline, he did not wish to imitate the episcopal forms of authority characteristic of the Catholic Church. Rather he wanted the church to be directed by a group of mature lay elders or presbyters, since all lay believers were considered priests. He judged that such an aristocratic body of mature elders was best qualified to enforce religious discipline. The chief characteristics of these elders, and indeed of all believers, should be that they are industrious, self-denying, and thrifty. Man is, for Calvin, helpless. He is in bondage to Satan and is saved solely by the grace of God, not his own efforts.

Calvin's followers were called Huguenots in France and Puritans in England. The Puritans were opposed to Anglicanism because it was episcopal (governed by bishops, instead of laypeople). In Scotland, John Knox (1515-1572) came to like Luther's teaching of justification by faith. When the Catholic Mary Tudor took the throne of England, he fled to Geneva and became Calvin's understudy. When Mary died in 1558 Knox returned to Scotland. Under his leadership, the Scottish government made Calvinism or Presbyterianism the state religion in 1560. Until his death in 1572, Calvin was the most powerful political and religious leader in Scotland.

The Calvinist churches are generally called Presbyterian ("ruled by elders") churches in English-speaking countries. Outside of the English-speaking countries most churches of this tradition are called Reformed churches. Reformed, when applied to a church, usually refers to a church that has been reformed according to the Biblical Gospel, that is, one that affirms the Bible as the basis of all Christian teaching. The Reformed churches have a tendency, for example, to admit only two sacraments, Baptism and the Lord's Supper, since these they judge to be the only ones explicitly mentioned in the Bible.

From the Lutheran and Reformed churches all the other Protestant communities descend as further reforms. The basic principle of the Reformation was *semper reformanda* (always being reformed). This principle encourages disagreement, renewal, and splintering.

4. Methodism

John Wesley (1703-1791), along with his brother Charles, attempted to deepen religious life and fervor within the traditional rituals of the Anglican Church. He formed organized societies who welcomed itinerant, or traveling, preachers, first in London, and then throughout the British Isles. These societies were meant to supplement, not replace, the worship of the Church of England. The Conferences of 1744-1747, that brought together representatives from these societies, formulated the main doctrinal emphases of Methodist preaching. These Conferences also consolidated the societies that had spread throughout England, Scotland and Ireland, and brought to them a strong family identity. *Minutes of Some Late Conversations between the Revd. Mr. Wesleys and Others*, published in 1749, established Methodism as a new religion. The itinerant preachers were so effective in their sermons that the people naturally desired to receive the sacraments from them. This soon led to the transformation of this movement of itinerant preachers who meant to supplement the religious life of the Anglican Church and led it in the direction of a separate church.

In 1752, and again in 1755, efforts were made by the Wesleys to get the traveling preachers to sign agreements never to leave the communion of the Church of England.

British immigrants brought Methodism to America, and the chief leader, who stayed even during the Revolutionary War, was Francis Asbury. He convinced the American Methodists who wanted to separate from John Wesley's leadership that they should remain in union with him. Paradoxically, this preservation of ties with Wesley eventually permitted him to help the Americans to establish the first independent church within Methodism. At the "Christmas Conference," held in Baltimore (1784-1785), with Wesley's approval, a new denomination was started, the Methodist Episcopal Church. Only in 1793 did the Wesleyan Methodist Society in England employ the word "church," and thus establish a separate entity from the Church of England.

Worship and Liturgy

Although all Protestants worship only one God, various denominations worship him in vastly different ways. Protestant liturgies, or worship services, vary from simple, informal meetings to elaborate ceremonies. Despite their many differences, however, most Protestant liturgies share the basic features of faith in the word of God, belief in sacraments, and the importance of the laity, or nonclergy.

Most Protestant liturgies stress preaching and hearing the word of God. Protestants believe that God is present in their midst and inspires faith in them when they read, hear, and discuss the Bible. For this reason, most Protestant services focus attention on the preacher and the sermon.

The various Protestant denominations disagree about the nature and number of sacraments, but most include at least two in their worship, baptism and communion. Baptism may involve water being poured or sprinkled on the head, or the person may be immersed totally in water. Many denominations practice infant baptism; in others, only individuals who are personally able to affirm their faith in Jesus Christ as their savior are baptized.

Communion, also called the Lord's Supper, is more symbolic in nature for many Protestants than it is for Roman Catholics and Orthodox Christians, who believe that the bread and wine they receive are actually the body and blood of Christ. Where Roman Catholics receive weekly or daily communion, most Protestant churches observe the ritual less often. Some observe it weekly or monthly; others observe it every three months.

Church Organization

Most Protestant churches stress the role of church members who are not clergy. Protestantism encourages people to take part in the liturgy through singing and prayer. This serves to establish a sense of community among the members of the congregation. The Society of Friends (Quakers) took this concept to its extreme, dispensing with all forms of clergy altogether. At a Quaker meeting, anyone who feels that he or she has received a message from God may speak up.

Observances

Some leaders of the Reformation, such as John Calvin, opposed the traditional church calendar of holy days, filled as it was with saints' days, transformed pagan feasts, and the worship of Mary. One of the first reforms was the abandonment of the cult of the saints and the worship of Mary and, thereby, most of the traditional feasts of the Roman Catholic church were discarded.

Protestant congregations today, however, do celebrate many of the traditional holy days of Christendom, with special emphasis on the seasons of Advent (the period beginning four Sundays before Christmas) and Lent (which takes place in the last winter months in preparation for Easter) and on the days of Christmas, Epiphany (January 6, commemorating the manifestation of Christ

Adventist	Mennonite
African Methodist Episcopal	Methodist
African Methodist Episcopal Zion	Moravian Church
Amanite	Mormon
Amish	National Baptist Convention
Assemblies of God	Pentecostal Churches
Baptist	Pentecostal Holiness Church
Brethren	Presbyterian
Christian Methodist Episcopal	Progressive National Baptist
Christian Reformed Church	Convention
Christian Scientist	Reformed Church in America
Church of God in Christ	Schwenkfelder
Church of the Nazarene	Seventh-day Adventist
Churches of God	Shaker
Congregationalist	Society of Friends (Quakers)
Disciples of Christ	Swedenborgian
Doukhobor	Unitarian Universalist Association
Hutterite	Unitarian
Jehovah's Witnesses	United Church of Canada
Lutheran	United Church of Christ

to the Gentiles in the persons of the Magi), Palm Sunday, Maundy (Holy) Thursday, Good Friday, Easter, and Pentecost Sunday.

Anglicanism and Its Beliefs

The development of Anglicanism came in several stages. In 1536, following the 1534 Act of Supremacy by which Henry VIII broke with the Roman Catholic church, Henry directed that a definition of faith and a book of common prayer be drawn up. With the publication of the "King's Book" in 1546, a creed was arrived at that was entirely Catholic except for its emphasis on the authority of the Bible and on justification by faith. During the reign of Henry's daughter Elizabeth I, Parliament drew up another definition of faith and revised the *Book of Common Prayer.* The articles of faith developed in Elizabeth's reign are still fundamental to the Anglican creed.

The church that evolved under Elizabeth was a compromise. It took its rules primarily from the teachings of Martin Luther, but it retained the ritual of the Roman Catholic church and modeled the church hierarchy on that of the Roman church—with the difference being the monarch instead of the pope as its head. Anglicans today often view themselves as a "bridge church" between Protestantism and Roman Catholicism.

Anglicans base their religion on Scripture, tradition, and reason. They believe in the ancient faith of Christianity as expressed in the Apostles' Creed and the Nicene Creed. The *Book of Common Prayer* is the collection of liturgy, prayers, and teachings used by the church, and this forms the basis for doctrine and discipline as well as worship. The *Book of Common Prayer,* the Bible, and a hymnal are the common elements in the various celebrations of the Anglican service.

Worship and Liturgy

The sacrament of the Holy Eucharist is the central act of worship in the Anglican tradition, as it is in Roman Catholicism and Eastern Orthodoxy. The liturgy recalls the story of Christ's sacrifice for the redemption of humankind each time it is offered.

Within the Episcopal church, the Anglican church in America, Episcopalians differ on how to interpret and practice their faith. High Churchmen believe in closely following the traditional practices of the church and in the church's authority. Broad Churchmen, or Liberals, have less strong feelings about tradition. They believe in expressing their faith in various ways, particularly through social action. Low Churchmen, or Evangelicals, emphasize the personal and biblical bases of faith.

Church Organization

Present-day Anglicans belong to churches that are part of a worldwide fellowship known as the Anglican communion. In addition to the Church of England, which was the first Anglican church and is the only one that is state-established, the Anglican communion includes the Church of Ireland, the Church of Wales, the Anglican Church of Canada, the Church of Australia, the Church of the Provinces of New Zealand, the Protestant

Episcopal Church in the United States of America (with missionary dioceses in South America and the Philippines), the Church of India, Pakistan, Burma, and Ceylon, the Church of South Africa, the Church of West Africa and of Central Africa, the Church of the West Indies, and the Holy Catholic Church of Japan.

Anglican churches are governed by a hierarchy of bishops, priests, and deacons, as is the Roman Catholic church. The archbishop of Canterbury is the spiritual leader of the Anglican church—and he claims a line that can be traced back through 120 archbishops of the English church to Saint Augustine of Canterbury in A.D. 597. He has, however, no jurisdiction outside his own diocese. Beginning in the 1900s, lay people have taken an increasingly important part in church affairs.

About every ten years, the Lambeth Conference of bishops meets in London. This conference serves mainly as a consulting and planning body and can only advise the churches it represents.

■ *The Reverend Barbara Harris, first woman bishop of the Episcopalian church, celebrates Mass in the Episcopalian diocese of Boston.*

Observances

Anglican Christians commemorate most of the traditional holy days of Christendom, with special emphasis on the Epiphany, Easter, the Ascension, Pentecost, and Christmas. In addition, Anglicans celebrate the following days:

- **Saint Augustine of Canterbury** (May 26): commemorates the saint who was instrumental in converting Britain to Christianity and who is considered the first archbishop of Canterbury
- **Saints Peter and Paul** (June 29): celebrates the martyrdom of the chief apostles of the Christian church
- **Saint Mary the Virgin** (August 15): Anglicans hold a high regard for the role of Mary in the redemption story
- **All Saints' Day** (November 1): celebrates the lives of those saints, known and unknown, whose witness to the faith touched the lives of others and who to this day continue to aid Christian pilgrims by their prayer and example.

■ **Founders of Some Christian Sects**

King Henry VIII of England
  Anglicanism
John Wesley
  Methodism
Martin Luther
  Lutheranism
John Calvin
  Presbyterianism
Ulrich Zwingli
  Anabaptists
Joseph Smith
  Church of Latter-Day Saints (Mormons)
Mary Baker Eddy
  Christian Scientists
Menno Simons
  Mennonites

CHAPTER 5

Rites
of Passage

Many Christians are usually baptized shortly after birth and confirmed when they are between eight and sixteen years old. When they get married, they usually do so in a church ceremony. When seriously ill, they receive the sacrament of the anointing of the sick, and a Mass of the resurrection follows their death. Such ceremonies as baptism, confirmation, marriage, and funerals are, in the language of today's sociologists, rites of passage, because they mark dramatic changes in human existence and celebrate the passing from one stage of life to another.

In Christian religious ceremonies, many of these celebrations of key events are called sacraments—they are signs of divine help or grace needed to live according to the full Christian demands of these stages of life. For instance, Christian marriage, as Saint Paul portrays it, commits the husband and wife to try to the best of their ability, with God's help, to live together for the rest of their lives. Their devotion to each other resembles Christ's love for the church—a love that led him to sacrifice his life for his beloved, the members of his church. No human being could live up to this example of Christ without special help or grace from

God. For the Christian, then, marriage is a sign of such a commitment of the spouses to live according to this example of Christ and an acknowledgment that they could not do so without special divine help. A sacrament, furthermore, means that God gives this grace or help with the conferral of the sacrament.

The most common rites of passage in and of themselves have little or nothing to do with religion. For example, graduating from high school or college, getting married and becoming a parent are all rites of passage that do not necessarily have religious significance for all individuals. But many of these benchmarks in life do have religious implications for believers. Marriage, for instance, demands that the couple imitate Christ's selfless love for one's spouse. Other rites, such as baptism and confirmation, are strictly religious rites. For Christians, elaborate rituals are celebrated at baptism, confirmation, marriage, and acceptance into holy orders, to signify the new responsibilities and their seriousness and to ask God for the assistance needed to fulfill the demands of these new states of life.

Most rites of passage help a person understand and accept the new role in life. They also serve as a sign to other people that the person should be treated in new ways that are appropriate to the new status. Christian sacramental rites of passage set up some parallel with Christ's life and show how Christian baptism, confirmation, marriage, or holy orders link Christians to Christ's life and example. They also offer to the Christian the divine assistance to live their life according to this higher ideal.

Most rites of passage, whether Christian or secular, have three stages: separation, transition, and incorporation. First, a participant in a rite of passage is separated from his or her previous status. In marriage, for example, this separation is often symbolized by a bridal shower or a bachelor party. In the transitional phase, the participant learns the behavior appropriate to the new status and undergoes the ceremony attached to it. Premarital counseling by a pastor and the wedding ceremony, which take place during a sacred and solemn period set apart from ordinary life, constitute this phase in the marriage rite. After the transitional period, the participant is formally incorporated, or initiated, into the new role.

Parallel to these rites of passage, but claiming a deeper meaning, is the description in Saint Paul's Letter to the Colossians of the passage rite in Christian baptism:

> *For when you were baptized, you were buried with Christ, and in baptism you were also raised with Christ through your faith in the active power of God, who raised him from death. . . . You have died with Christ and are set free from the ruling spirits of the universe. Why, then, do you live as though you belonged to this world? . . . You have been raised to life with Christ, so set your hearts on the things that are in heaven, where Christ sits on his throne at the right side of God. Keep your minds fixed on things there, not on things here on earth.*

> *You must put to death, then, the earthly desires at work in you, such as sexual immorality, indecency, lust, evil passions and greed . . . . You are the people of God; he loved you and chose you for his own. So then, you must clothe yourselves with compassion, kindness, humility, gentleness, and patience . . . . Christ's message in all its richness must live in your hearts.* (Col. 2.12-3.16)

Participants in most rites of passage wear special garments to symbolize the change they are undergoing. Examples of such dress are graduation caps and gowns, white dresses and veils worn by girls at their First Communion and the wedding gowns and formal attire worn by many brides and grooms.

A discussion of the Christian rites of passage that occur with the birth of a child (baptism), during childhood (confirmation), at adulthood (matrimony and holy orders), and at the time of a person's serious illness and death (anointing of the sick) follows.

Baptism

The first rite of passage experienced by most Christians is baptism. For Roman Catholics, Orthodox Christians, and many Protestants, baptism occurs within a few days after birth. Christian baptism marks the entry of an individual into Christian society and association with the Christian faith. The water that is used during the ceremony symbolizes both cleansing from sin and the living, flowing waters of new life in Christ. Baptism is thus the foundation of Christian life, its initiation into the soul of the baptized.

Various passages in the Bible referring to baptism have led to differences in practice and belief among the various Christian denominations. Regardless of how baptism is carried out, however, the uniting factor is the use of water as a sign and agent of spiritual cleansing.

Most Christian churches practice baptism in the name of the Trinity, in accordance with Jesus' instructions to his disciples: "Go ye therefore, and teach all nations, baptizing them in the name of the Father, and of the Son, and of the Holy Spirit." (Matt. 28.19) Some groups, such as Eastern Orthodox Christians and Baptists, practice baptism after the manner of the early Christians, by total immersion in water. Roman Catholic baptism usually involves the pouring of water over the infant's head. Other groups may baptize by sprinkling the infant with water or by the minister's dipping his or her fingers in water and placing them on the child's head.

Although some Protestant denominations, such as the Quakers (members of the Society of Friends) and Christian Scientists, do not practice baptism, it is usually viewed by Christians as being necessary for salvation:

> The man who believes in it and accepts baptism will be saved; the man who refuses to believe in it will be condemned.   (Mark 16.16)

> No one can enter into God's Kingdom without being begotten of water and Spirit.   (John 3.5)

Some Christian denominations call baptism a law, and others call it a sacrament. Some groups baptize a person so that he or she may thereby receive the Holy Spirit, in accordance with the legal demands of the apostle Peter: "Repent, and be baptized every one of you in the name of Jesus Christ for the remission of sins, and ye shall receive the gift of the Holy Spirit." (Acts 2:38) Others baptize because they believe that the person who is cleansed

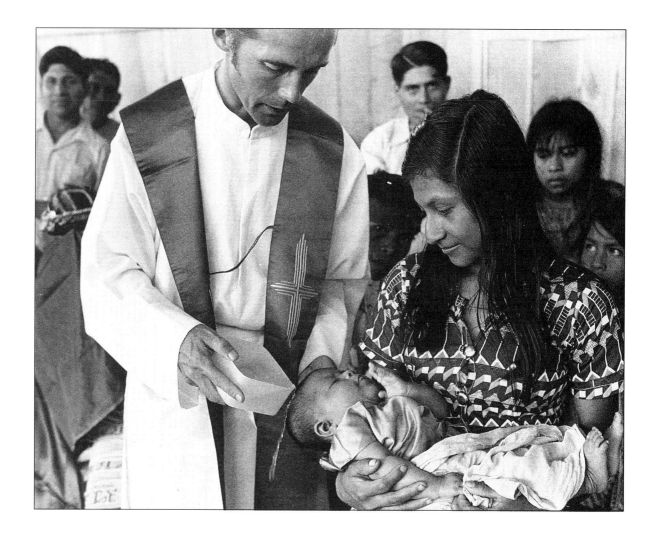

by the water is also cleansed spiritually by God's grace or power. For them, water is a sign or sacrament of spiritual cleansing.

Some Christian groups—in particular, Roman Catholics and Anglicans—require godparents, or sponsors, to be present at a baptism in addition to the child's parents. Roman Catholic law actually forbids baptism without the presence of godparents, except when a newborn child is in danger of death. The godparents promise to sponsor the child's religious training in case its parents for any reason are not able to do so. Most Protestant churches make the parents alone responsible for their child's

■ A priest baptizes a young child by pouring water on the child's head, while saying, "I baptize you in the name of the Father, and of the Son, and of the Holy Spirit."

religious upbringing, and the position of godparent is largely honorary and carries no responsibilities.

Since Christian baptism is a sign of conversion—that is, of the turning of a person's life toward Jesus Christ—the baptism of adults throughout Christian history has been preceded by a long period of introduction into the faith. Before the baptism of a child, a baptismal conversation takes place with the parents and godparents, who will later introduce the child to the faith. The parents and godparents, answering for the child, must renounce Satan, the evil one, and confess faith in God, the almighty Father, in Jesus Christ, the Son of God, and in the Holy Spirit.

Christians believe that by being united with Christ through baptism, they are also united with all other Christians. Through baptism a community is created that goes beyond all natural boundaries of nations, cultures, races, social classes, and sex. According to Saint Paul:

> *All of you who have been baptized into Christ have clothed yourselves with him. There does not exist among you Jew or Greek, slave or freeman, male or female. All are one in Christ Jesus.* (Gal. 3.27-28)

Christening, or naming an infant, often takes place formally at the time of baptism. The custom of bestowing a name on the newly baptized child dates from early Christian times, when a person took a new name at baptism. The new name was the name of a saint who was to serve as a model and inspiration during life for the person baptized.

Some Protestant denominations reject the Catholic and Orthodox practice of infant baptism. Their belief is that a person cannot enter the church until he or she is old enough to make his or her own declaration of faith in Jesus Christ. Baptists in particular view this rite of passage as giving people participation in the mission of Jesus—through baptism, every believer in effect becomes a priest, required to bear witness to Jesus.

Confirmation

Another rite of passage that takes place at different ages for members of different Christian churches is confirmation. In the

Eastern Orthodox church, confirmation, or chrismation, immediately follows the baptism of an infant. As a rite of passage, confirmation signals the movement of a Christian into full membership in the church. Oil is used to anoint the forehead and other parts of the body of the infant as the words "the seal of the gift of the Holy Spirit" are spoken.

Confirmation is the principal rite of passage that a Roman Catholic child undergoes. Through this solemn rite, the child becomes a full member of the church. One symbol of this maturity is the strike on the cheek by the confirming bishop. The blow is a sign of the trials one might experience in living as a mature Christian. The sacrament of confirmation confers the divine assistance or grace that is necessary for withstanding whatever trials of faith might appear in life.

Preparation of a child for confirmation is viewed as the task of the entire community, but in particular of the child's parents and godparents. Children who are to be confirmed study their faith in small groups. The principal means of learning is the catechism, a system of questions and answers. Common experiences and community tasks of dedicated service support the lessons learned through the catechism.

The bishop, the traditional celebrant of confirmation, places his hand on the head of the child being confirmed and signs the child's forehead in the form of a cross with chrism, or holy oil. Oil is a symbol of strength, and this anointing is a sign that God will provide those being confirmed with the strength they will need to face the trials of faith that might come to them through life.

Marriage

As a rite of passage, marriage moves a man and woman from the unmarried state to the state of being one together. Christian marriage is identified with the sacred union of Christ and his church. Through the sacrament of matrimony, the couple is called to imitate Christ's love for his people, the church, especially as a sign of the sacrificial form of love that Christ showed in his freely chosen suffering and death for humankind.

Christians usually prepare for marriage by receiving pastoral counseling. It is the duty of the pastor to ensure that the couple is aware of the civil and Christian responsibilities they will face as a married couple and as parents.

In the traditional religious ceremony, the bridesmaids and ushers walk slowly down the center aisle of the church to the altar. They stand on either side of the altar throughout the ceremony, the ushers at the groom's side and the bridesmaids at the bride's side. The groom enters through a side door and waits for the bride at the altar. The bride then walks down the aisle with her

■ At the wedding ceremony, the bride and groom are reminded of the Christian ideals of marriage, and are asked to share their lives as examples of God's love for all human beings.

father or father and mother. The bride usually wears a white dress and veil, and she carries a bouquet. When they reach the altar, the father (or the father and the mother), according to ceremonial rule, entrusts the bride to the groom. At the altar, the bride and groom exchange marriage vows and accept each other as husband and wife. The groom puts a wedding ring on the ring finger of the bride's left hand (in some countries, the traditional wedding ring finger is on the right hand), and the bride may also give the groom a ring. After the ceremony, the bride and groom kiss and make their way out of the church down the main aisle, followed by the rest of the wedding party.

Infinite variations exist on the traditional ceremony. Music is often played during the procession and recession. Sometimes the couple may write their own wedding service. Songs, poetry, and readings from the Bible may be part of the service. Attendants may include flower girls and ring bearers as well as bridesmaids and ushers. The bride may walk down the aisle unaccompanied, or accompanied by both of her parents, or the bride and groom may enter together. Many Roman Catholic weddings take place during a Mass, and the bride and groom and members of the wedding party and the congregation receive Holy Communion.

In contrast to the elaborate and ceremonial nuptial Mass of a Roman Catholic couple is the simple wedding of members of the Society of Friends (Quakers), who have no clergy. Quakers marry at a public gathering where they declare their commitment to each other.

A wedding is usually followed by the sharing of food and drink with guests, once again a sign that marriage itself will demand on the part of the couple a life of generosity toward one another and to others. The celebration can be a simple buffet in the church hall or a lavish party with a band and a full-course dinner. The sharing with others is the important aspect of this part of a wedding.

Ordination or Holy Orders (Adulthood)

During his lifetime, Jesus selected disciples to help him carry out his mission to spread the gospel. The 12 apostles were not his only disciples. At one time, he sent out 70. After his resurrection,

Christian doctrine teaches, Jesus confirmed his disciples' special calling and mission to preach, baptize, and forgive sins. From the earliest beginnings of the Christian church, certain men and women have felt a special calling to serve God.

Preparation for a life of dedicated service in a church of any denomination involves years of study in a theological seminary, which is a school for training members of the clergy. In addition to academic subjects, seminary students usually take comprehensive classes in the doctrines, sacred writings, history, and philosophy of their church. They may also study practical subjects, such as pastoral psychology and counseling.

The ceremonies associated with ordination into the clergy vary according to the religious denomination. In the Roman Catholic and Eastern Orthodox churches, the taking of holy orders is a sacrament. The man ordained is enabled to act "in the person of Christ." His task is to preach and teach, to confer the sacraments, and to lead the people who are entrusted to him. In the Roman Catholic Church, priestly ordination also carries an obligation to celibacy—the duty to remain unmarried and to live in perfect chastity, that is, to refrain from sexual intercourse. In the Orthodox Church, priests may marry, but they must choose to do so before they are ordained priests. Women likewise dedicate themselves to a life of service within the church as nuns and lay ministers. Some Christian churches allow women to join the clergy; in others—particularly the Roman Catholic, Eastern Orthodox, and Anglican churches—such a practice is strictly forbidden.

Anointing of the Sick

The last statement of the *Apostles' Creed*, the traditional affirmation of the Christian faith, reads:

> *I believe in the Holy Spirit; the holy Catholic Church;*
> *the Communion of Saints; the Forgiveness of sins; the*
> *resurrection of the body; and Life everlasting.*

Belief in the resurrection of Christ and that through faith in Christ humankind can be resurrected to eternal life is at the heart of Christian belief. When death is seen as a passage to eternal life, it can be accepted and even welcomed.

■ *Nuns, or sisters, are an important part of the life of the Catholic church. They serve as teachers, directors or nurses in hospitals, professors in universities, and leaders in many of the social works of the church.*

Christian tradition calls death "the end of a person's pilgrim state" or "the end of a person's life as a wayfarer." All one's life, in a sense, is viewed as a preparation for death. Death is the end of a person's responsibility for shaping his or her earthly life and working to achieve salvation through the grace of God.

Catholic belief specifies four last things: death, judgment, hell, and heaven. At the moment of death, Catholic doctrine teaches, people are judged according to the way they have led their lives. The souls of those who die in mortal sin, unrepentant and unforgiven, will go to hell. The souls of those who have repented their sins and have been forgiven are in a state of grace and will be received into the presence of God in heaven. Those who die without grave sin, but who have venial sins, or lesser sins, on their soul for which they have not made recompense, are sent to purgatory. There the soul is cleansed and readied for union with God in heaven. This judgment at the time of death is known as the particular judgment. The Last or Final Judgment, when the fate of human beings will be decided for all eternity, will be held at the Second Coming of Christ.

According to Christian belief, at the end of the world, Christ will come again, and the souls of all people will be reunited with their bodies. Then, according to the Bible:

The Son of man shall send forth his angels, and they shall
gather out of his kingdom all things that offend, and them
which do iniquity, and shall cast them into a furnace of
fire: there shall be wailing and gnashing of teeth. Then
shall the righteous shine forth as the sun in the kingdom
of their Father. (Matt. 13.41-43)

Although the Catholic, Anglican, and Orthodox sacrament of anointing of the sick, or extreme unction, is not limited to people who are dying, it plays a role in the preparation of a person for death. The sacrament is administered by a priest, who anoints the sense organs of the seriously sick or dying person with consecrated oil and says, "Through this holy anointing may the Lord in his love and mercy help you with the grace of the Holy Spirit. Amen. May the Lord who frees you from sin save you and raise you up. Amen." The sacrament bestows grace on the person who receives it, removing sin and its consequences. It completes the penance of Christian life and assures a new life.

The final part of the rite of passage that is death is the funeral. Although funeral customs may vary, many of the same practices are carried out throughout the Christian world: public announcement of the death, preparation of the body, funeral services, a procession, burial or cremation (burning of the body), and mourning.

Preparation of the body usually consists of laying out and washing the corpse and sometimes anointing it with oils. In the United States, where burial may be delayed for several days, most bodies are preserved by a special process called embalming to retard decay. If the body is to be viewed by mourners, makeup will be applied to give the corpse a more lifelike appearance. The body is then dressed in new clothes or wrapped in a cloth called a shroud and placed in a coffin, or casket.

During the period between death and burial, relatives and friends come to view the body, if it is displayed, and to express their sympathies to the family. In some countries, a wake, or a watch, may be held. Traditionally, the wake allows the mourners to pray for the dead and to console the living in their loss.

Funeral services vary widely and may include prayers and hymns or other music. They also include speeches called eulogies, in which those who knew the dead person will often recall telling incidents from the person's life and praise the person for his or her good nature or accomplishments. After the service, a procession of cars usually follows the hearse carrying the corpse to a cemetery. A final, brief ceremony is held at the grave before the body is buried or cremated. After the funeral, the mourners often return with the family of the dead person to their home or to another place and share food and consolation.

A funeral fills important emotional needs for the family and friends of the dead person. It focuses attention on their grief and provides a public ceremony that helps them acknowledge and accept their loss. It also gives them an opportunity to express their feelings and discharge their grief.

CHAPTER 6

The Impact
of Christianity

Throughout its history, Christianity has had an impact on every aspect of human life in the lands where it has been practiced. The extent of its influence has been greater or less in different countries and in different historical periods, but its greatest influence was probably felt in Europe during the Middle Ages, or as it is sometimes called, the Age of Faith. The influence of Christianity, and indeed, religion in general, has diminished in recent years, causing some people to believe that we are living in a secular or nonreligious and worldly age.

Yet even today the Christian influence is all around us. There is probably not a town in the United States that does not have at least one Christian church. Some of the most magnificent buildings in important cities are the great cathedrals of the Roman Catholic church. The stars and mangers that appear among the colored lights and other decorations that adorn streets, homes, and public buildings throughout the country at Christmastime are a reminder that this holiday, as secular as it may have become for many, is still a celebration of the birth of Christ. Moreover, despite the constitutional separation of church and state in the

United States, many of the laws and ethical expectations of our society reflect Christian origins. What follows is a concise survey of the influence of Christianity on daily life, education, art, architecture, music, and literature in the United States and around the world.

Daily Life

In an early chapter of the Acts of the Apostles, Luke tells us that the followers of Christ in Jerusalem continued to gather in community and that they shared their belongings with one another. "They sold their property and possessions and distributed the money among all, according to what each one needed." (Acts 3.45) In many ways, during the earliest days of Christianity, the Christians must not have stood out that much from other Jews who attached themselves to a particular teacher. They went to the synagogue, looked like the other Jews, and in many cases followed the Jewish celebrations, even if they gave to them a new Christian meaning or interpretation.

As Christianity spread among the Greek communities, Christians could not be distinguished from the rest of the human race. Christianity was not associated with the customs or language of a particular people. Rather, Christians have inhabited all places, and they have lived life as it was lived in their respective countries. Still, Christians throughout the ages have argued about what makes them different from the other people. One characteristic that distinguishes Christians is their philosophy of love. Christians are called to love God with all their heart and soul and to love their neighbors as they love themselves. The Christian God is a loving God, and Christ taught, above all else, compassion and forgiveness.

Christian love is not something true Christians engage in every Sunday and forget about during the rest of the week. Rather, it is an integral part of the daily life of every Christian. Christians, according to their faith, live their everyday lives with Christian ideals in mind. They manifest their love in activities such as the corporal works of mercy mentioned toward the end of Matthew's Gospel: feeding the hungry, clothing the naked, visiting the sick and imprisoned, welcoming strangers, and burying the dead.

In the United States today, Christians generally practice their religion privately, alone or with their families, or in church on Sunday (Saturday for Seventh-day Adventists). During Lent, many Christians traditionally fast or do not eat meat on certain days; and special services may be held on Ash Wednesday, Holy Thursday, or Good Friday. Religious services are also held on important Christian holy days such as Easter and Christmas. Most Christians, however, live their lives in the same way as other citizens. They wear no special clothing and rarely follow any special dietary regulations. Some children may attend parochial, or church-run, schools, but most attend public schools. For the most part, there is no significant difference between the Christian population and the general population in the life they live; it is rather the manner in which—or purpose for which—

■ *People kneeling in prayer in the pews of their parish church.*

they live that might distinguish them from others. This, however, is usually not a very visible difference.

A few Christian groups, because of their particular beliefs, live quite differently than their neighbors do. The Amish, a special group of Mennonites, for example, teach separation from the world. Farming and personal simplicity is their way of life. The Amish do not use electricity, the telephone, or machinery of any sort. They plow their land with horses and ride in horse-driven buggies. The dress of the Amish is simple and employs somber colors. The women wear long, plain dresses and bonnets; the men wear shirts without ties, dark pants, and wide-brimmed hats. Married men do not shave or trim their beards. Academic education for Amish children generally ends at the eighth grade, for in their lives as farmers, they will require no more formal schooling.

Many ministers, priests, monks, and nuns at times have worn distinctive dress outside their religious houses. These distinctive garments were meant to set them apart as a group who were in a special way committed to dedicating their lives to God. Unlike these special groups, however, most Christians dress in the various styles of the times, in no way reflecting their religious beliefs.

Education

Christ's first apostles were not scholars. They were fishermen. Christ did not think that scholars were particularly qualified to preach the gospel. Some early Christians, like Tertullian in the early third century, preferred a Christianity that was characterized by the simplicity of the fisherman rather than by the intellectual investigation of the scholar. To Tertullian, and some other Christians, the wisdom of this world seemed to undermine the teachings of the gospel. For example, the schools of the classical world of Greece and Rome used for their basic texts the works of writers such as Homer and Virgil, with their tales of vengeful and sensual pagan gods and stories of heroes who seemed to lack many Christian virtues, especially the virtue of humility. There were in fact many temptations for Christians to become anti-intellectual, since the early intellectual world was so pagan.

Yet many resisted this temptation. Ignatius of Antioch realized that his search for meaning through the study of the pagan classics was not satisfying. He was looking for something more than these classics provided, and so he turned to a study of the gospels.

Other Christians found the teachings of the gospels to be misunderstood or misrepresented by opponents. They realized that they needed skills in logic and rhetoric to refute them. Secular learning of these subjects was therefore very useful, indeed necessary, if Christians wanted to refute their attackers.

Christians saw the need for studying the traditional subjects of the seven liberal arts that the pagans studied—grammar, rhetoric, dialectic, arithmetic, geometry, music and astronomy— to defend and explain the teachings of the gospels. Saint Augustine, in his work *On Christian Teaching*, argued strongly that these works were key to understanding, explaining, and defending the Christian Scriptures.

Augustine saw intellectual needs that Tertullian did not see, and, in effect, through Augustine's appeal a certain kind of Christian intellectualism began to develop. In the Greek world, parallel disputes took place, and Basil and Gregory of Nazianzen won the day by arguing for the importance of study within their Greek Christian communities. King Charlemagne of the Holy Roman Empire, in his educational reforms, fostered the development of centers of learning in his palaces, and his initiatives also fostered education in the monasteries and cathedrals. Cathedral schools, centered in towns, were more available to people who did not intend to pursue church positions. As more towns were established and more cathedrals were built, these schools increased in number throughout Europe, especially in France. Many of the great universities of Europe developed from such schools.

During the Reformation of the 1500s, Protestant sections of Europe began to establish elementary schools to teach the children of common citizens to read the Bible in their native languages. The Roman Catholic church, as part of its own reform movement, also expanded its educational activities during this period. Schools were established for Catholic children in which they were taught in their own languages.

Most colonists who came to the Americas from Europe set up the kinds of schools they had known in their homelands. The teaching of reading was fostered in colonial New England in the belief that by knowing the Scriptures, people would be able to defeat the power of the devil. Both Protestants and Roman Catholics established and supported their own schools. Most of these were elementary schools where reading, writing, and religion were taught. Later, secondary schools and even small colleges were founded by churches, primarily to train young men for the ministry. Many of these colleges have developed in the twentieth century into large and respected universities.

Art and Architecture

Although the Christian church did not continue many of the ritual laws of the Jewish people, they did cling to the Ten Commandments. The first commandment prohibits the making of images of anything in heaven or on earth that could serve as idols. This prohibition made the early Christians hesitate to make any images. The earliest works of Christian art began appearing in the third century in the form of mural paintings in burial chambers, such as the Roman catacombs. The subjects of these paintings included Christ's early miracle of the multiplication of the loaves and fishes and scenes based on other biblical stories.

As the church came out of hiding after years of persecution, works of Christian art began to appear. This can be seen in the beautiful mosaics that survive in the churches of Ravenna, Italy, or the impressive illuminations in early manuscripts in the Vatican library. Before monarchs, lords, and wealthy merchants began to patronize artists during the Renaissance, almost all great art was religious art, commissioned by and for the church.

By the 500s, a distinct style of art and architecture had developed in the Byzantine Empire. Byzantine art was dedicated to portraying the doctrines of Christianity. In the domed churches of Byzantium, tapestries, mosaics, paintings, and murals recounting the life of Christ and the careers of saints and martyrs adorned every surface. The highest achievement of Byzantine architecture was the great cathedral, Hagia Sophia, in Constantinople. Its style—a huge central dome set on a square base—became a

■ The combination of religion and education is well indicated in this link-up of the alphabet, vowel and combined consonant sounds, and the Our Father. Such basic instruments as the horn book provided both religious and literary instruction in the American colonies.

■ *The church of St. Apollonaris in Ravenna, Italy offers one of the earliest mosaics in the Latin Christian work. This particular work represents Jesus Christ as the good shepherd caring for his spiritual sheep.*

common feature of Byzantine architecture. The impression made by this church is conveyed by the court poet Paul Silentiary:

> *When the first gleam of light, rosy-armed, driving away the dark shadows, leapt from arch to arch, then all hymned their songs of prayer and praise; it seemed to them as if the mighty arches were set in heaven. And above all rises into the immeasurable air the great helmet, which, bending over like the radiant heavens, embraces the church. . . .*

The golden stream of glittery rays pours down and strikes the eyes of men, so they can scarcely bear to look. . . . Thus through the spaces of the great church come rays of light, expelling clouds of care, filling the mind with promise, showing the way to the living God. . . .Whoever sets foot within this sacred place, would live there forever, and his eyes well with tears of joy.

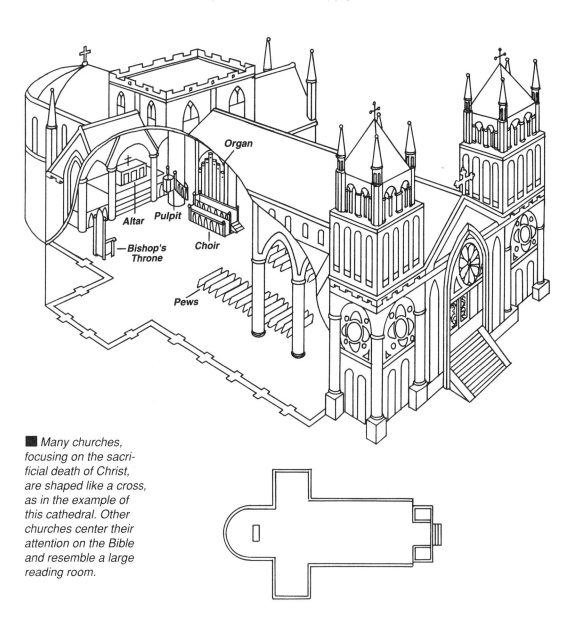

Organ

Altar Pulpit

Bishop's
Throne

Choir

Pews

■ *Many churches, focusing on the sacrificial death of Christ, are shaped like a cross, as in the example of this cathedral. Other churches center their attention on the Bible and resemble a large reading room.*

The Middle Ages in Europe was a period of deep religious faith. The church became the period's greatest patron of the arts, building churches and monasteries, decorating them with paintings, and filling them with altars, candelabra, and screens made of wood or iron. The frescoes of the l4th-century Italian painter Giotto and the stained glass of Chartres, for example, are visible reminders of this age of glory for Christian art.

Architects in the early part of the Middle Ages built churches that were based on the style that had been developed in the era of Rome's greatness. This Romanesque architecture was not of less quality than that which came before, but took on fresh creative forms. The more definitely Christian form of architecture is found later in the Middle Ages with the development of majestic Gothic cathedrals, such as Chartres, with arches and towers that seemed to soar to heaven. These cathedrals were intended to inspire a mood of reverence among worshipers, lifting their hearts to the heavens above. The invention of the flying buttress to support the soaring vault of the Gothic cathedral freed the walls for windows. Magnificent stained glass windows became the principal form of internal decoration in these cathedrals. As they knelt before richly carved altars, surrounded by beautiful images, bathed in colored light that had filtered through the stained glass windows, medieval worshipers must have felt both awed and uplifted.

Even though much art during the Renaissance began to be sponsored by nonchurch patrons, and increasingly artists were creating paintings and sculpture for private enjoyment, still some of the greatest works of religious art were created during this period. Pope Julius II made Rome an important artistic center. Among the great works of art he commissioned was the painting of the ceiling of the Sistine Chapel in the Vatican by Michelangelo. Other famous artists of the time included Raphael and Leonardo da Vinci.

The Reformation brought lean days for art in northern Europe. The Catholic church, fighting for its life in a series of religious wars, had neither the time nor the money to sponsor the work of artists. Under the influence of the developing Protestant churches, the demand for religious art lessened and visual art in general came under suspicion as leading to idolatry, the religious worship of idols. The Lutheran churches ignored art; the Calvinist churches condemned it. Only in the Netherlands did art survive the Reformation.

For the Reformed community, the church building was important only in its function as a place for the congregation to gather for services. When Roman Catholic churches were converted to use by Reformed communities, statues and even stained glass windows were often removed and destroyed. When Reformists began to build churches of their own, they used simple geometric designs that permitted the congregation to gather around the pulpit and table that had replaced the Catholic altar.

In southern Europe, the Catholic church was attempting to counter the charges of immorality and idolatry that had begun the Reformation. All church painting was strictly regulated. Pope Pius V went so far as to order clothing added to the nude figures Michelangelo had painted in the Sistine Chapel!

The lasting influence of the Reformation on the art world was that it pushed the production of art more into the secular arena. Whereas the medieval artist's patron had been the church, the artist of the Reformation and thereafter was sponsored by monarchs, princes, and the wealthy. Scenes from daily life replaced religious scenes as the primary focus of painting, while architects turned their talents to the design of palaces and great houses rather than cathedrals. From their former status as anonymous servants of the church, artists became professionals who proudly signed the pictures they painted.

Music

Christianity played an important part in the early growth of classical music. However, this was not the first influence Christianity had on music. The oldest known Christian form of music was plainsong, a simple form of vocal music that was used in early Christian church services. Plainsong was so called because a soloist or choir sang the melody without instrumental accompaniment or harmony. Plainsong developed gradually from early Jewish religious music, and much of it was set to the words of the Psalms, lyrical poems from the Old Testament. The most important type of plainsong was Gregorian chant, developed during the reign of Pope Gregory I (590-604). In the early Middle Ages, music was almost entirely in the service of the liturgy or public worship of the Church.

During the period of the Byzantine Empire, music began to play an increasing role in the liturgy of the Eastern church. About the end of the fifth century, Romanus, a Greek monk, composed the words and music of hymns that still form part of the Greek liturgy.

During the 11th century, an Italian monk named Guido d'Arezzo revolutionized the teaching of music. He developed a system of notation and a method of sight-reading. Another great musical innovation of the 11th century was polyphony—the putting together of two or more voices harmoniously. In the 1300s, the French composer Guillaume de Machaut wrote the first polyphonic setting for the entire Roman Catholic Mass.

■ Brightly illuminated manuscripts of the Middle Ages often contained the books of the Bible. This one, however, carries the words and plain-song chant sung by the priest at mass.

Many forms of classical music were created for church services. Most choral music in particular has been written for religious services. The principal form of such choral music is the mass, a series of pieces composed for a Catholic worship service. The earliest masses were written for small, unaccompanied choruses. Later composers—including Bach, Beethoven, and Schubert—wrote masses with parts for vocal soloists and orchestral accompaniment. The requiem, which is a special mass composed for funerals, also frequently involves choral singing. Important requiems were written by such composers as Mozart, Berlioz, and Verdi.

A hymn is a song of praise, and most hymns glorify God. Since biblical times, Jews have used the Psalms of the Old Testament as hymns. Today, both Jews and Christians sing hymns during their religious services. Until the 1500s, most Christian hymns were sung in Latin. During the Reformation, however, many churches began to conduct religious services in their national language. Martin Luther, a German leader of the Reformation, wrote several original hymns in German and translated many Latin hymns. During the 1700s, several hymnists broke the tradition of basing hymns on the Psalms, and thousands of original hymns were composed, some of which are still sung today.

Another form of music that developed under the influence of the Christian religion is the oratorio, a musical composition that uses soloists, chorus, and orchestra. The subject is usually taken from the Bible, and the first and most popular subject was the Passion, or sufferings of Christ. Perhaps the most famous oratorio is Bach's *Passion According to Saint Matthew*. Handel was the greatest writer of oratorios, of which he composed 15. The best known is *The Messiah*, the singing of which has become a Christmas tradition throughout the Christian world.

The influence of Christianity on music has extended into the late 20th century. Major works have been inspired by Christian motifs, such as conductor-composer Leonard Bernstein's *Mass*, Benjamin Britten's *War Requiem*, and Gian Carlo Menotti's opera *Amahl and the Night Visitors*. The musicals *Joseph and the Amazing Technicolor Dreamcoat*, *Godspell*, and *Jesus Christ Superstar* were successful attempts to retell scriptural stories in a contemporary musical style. These productions, aimed primarily at young people who might be more comfortable with contemporary music than with the more traditional oratorio form, were box-office hits.

Literature

From the third century, Christian authors, such as Tertullian (160-230), Saint Jerome (347-420), and Saint Augustine (354-430), were the most important writers of the day. It was as the language of the church—no longer of the Roman Empire—that Latin was to remain alive and vigorous up to the end of the Middle Ages.

After the fall of Rome, many European monasteries were founded by missionaries from Ireland, where Christianity and classical learning had been preserved. Irish monasteries reintroduced the Catholic faith into areas of Europe where it was unknown. With them they brought their libraries, both classical and Christian, which had remained safe in Ireland. The monasteries sheltered whatever learning Europe possessed in the early Middle Ages. Monastery libraries contained not only Bibles, biblical commentaries, and books required for liturgical services, but also the classics of ancient Greece and Rome that otherwise would have been lost forever. Monasteries also fostered the emergence of literature in the vernacular, the local languages as opposed to Latin. The supreme instance of vernacular literature is the *Divine Comedy* of Dante, in which he uses biblical and Christian imagery to transform the epic form of the Roman poet Virgil's *Aeneid* into a great Christian epic.

A wealth of literature was produced from the beginning of the fifth to the seventeenth century in Europe, and many of the greatest works were written by Christians. Although some of these works, such as the records of monasteries compiled by Christian monks during the Middle Ages, were merely records of monastic foundations, others, such as the history of England written by a British monk called the Venerable Bede (673-735), were masterpieces. Bede wrote many works on science, grammar, history, and theology.

One of the great classics of early English literature, Geoffrey Chaucer's *Canterbury Tales*, came out of the medieval tradition of pilgrimages. Chaucer's tales relate the adventures of a group of pilgrims of all classes on their way to the shrine in Canterbury of the murdered archbishop Thomas Becket.

In the beginning of the Reformation, theological writings were the main focus of literary activity. Reform writers delved primarily into the meaning of the Bible and wrote treatises and commentaries in which they gave their interpretations of the Biblical texts. They strongly criticized non-Biblical works as products of self-centered men. However, two great works of imagination produced in the Reformed tradition stand out both for their own worth and as examples of faith. These are John Milton's *Paradise Lost* and John Bunyan's *Pilgrim's Progress.*

Christianity and the Theater

Christianity's influence on the theater was at first negative. In Rome, many forms of theater were popular—tragedy, comedy, farce, and pantomime. Most of these performances were offensive to the early Christians, however, and as Christianity grew more powerful, the Roman theater declined. In the 400s, actors were excommunicated from the church, and Roman theater came to an end not long afterward. The last known theatrical performance in ancient Rome was in 533.

The rebirth of drama began in the 900s when priests and choirboys began to act out short plays as part of the worship service, especially in the church's attempt to make the gospels "come alive". A large body of plays grew up around the resurrection, the Christmas story, and other biblical events. The language of these plays was the language of the church, Latin.

In the 1300s, plays moved outdoors and began to be produced and acted by nonreligious organizations, such as trade and craft guilds or trade associations. They came to be called mystery plays from another name for these guilds, masteries or mysteries, or Corpus Christi plays because most were presented during the feast of Corpus Christi in late May or in June.

Mystery plays were staged outdoors on large carts called pageant wagons. A wagon was drawn through a town to various places where spectators stood in the street or watched from nearby houses. The actors were townspeople, most of whom belonged to the guilds that produced the plays. Mystery plays were presented in cycles of several related dramas over a period of one or two days. Each guild in a town was responsible for one episode or play.

Although mystery plays dramatized scenes from the Old and New Testaments, many included comical scenes, often involving the devil or fools. Biblical scenes were often combined with references to local places and events. The plays were written in verse and were organized very loosely. Cycles of mystery plays from England, France, Italy, and Spain have survived to the present.

Miracle plays, which developed out of mystery plays, were also popular during the Middle Ages. Like mystery plays, they were presented initially as part of Catholic church services but lost the approval of the church. After being driven out of the churches and into the streets, miracle plays were performed by trade guild members on feast days. Miracle plays dramatized events from the life of the Virgin Mary or the lives of saints. The action of most of these plays reached a climax in a miracle performed by the saint—which gave them their name.

Another form of medieval drama, the morality play, was first produced in England in the 1400s. Like the mystery and miracle play, the morality play developed from religious pageants. Its purpose was to teach a lesson or to show the eternal struggle between good and evil for control of human beings. The morality play became more fully developed than other types of medieval drama, growing from a fairly simple religious play to a secular entertainment performed by professional companies of actors. While morality plays were primarily serious, the characters of Vice and the Devil were usually treated in a comical way to make the play more entertaining to the audience. The clowns and fools in the plays of William Shakespeare developed out of the comic characters in morality plays. *Everyman*, a favorite morality play of the 1500s, is still performed annually at a music and drama festival in Salzburg, Austria.

In Spain during the Middle Ages, drama became an important means of religious teaching. Spanish religious plays combined elements of the mystery, or cycle, play and the morality play. Human and supernatural characters were mingled with

symbolic figures, such as Grace, Pleasure, and Sin. Dramatists took their stories from both secular and religious sources, adapting them to uphold church teachings. Like the English mystery plays, the Spanish plays were performed outdoors on wagons.

During the late Middle Ages, European townspeople and villagers often staged Passion plays, plays that depict the suffering, crucifixion, and death of Jesus Christ. By taking part in a Passion play, townspeople also participated in the drama of Christ's last days on earth. The Passion play tradition continues to the present in towns in southern Germany, western Austria, and Switzerland. The most famous one is held every ten years in the Bavarian town of Oberammergau.

The Reformation had both positive and negative effects on the history of drama. The positive effect was its promotion of the vernacular over the use of Latin. The use of local languages eventually led to the development of national drama in many countries. Theater flourished in England and France. England, however, experienced the negative effect of the Reformation when the Puritans gained control of Parliament in the 1640s and prohibited theatrical performances. The Puritan government closed the English theaters in 1642. They remained closed until the restoration of King Charles II in 1660. Puritan disapproval of theatrical performances was also part of the history of the theater in the United States.

CHAPTER *7*

Christianity Facing New Challenges

*T*he world has changed dramatically since the days of the early Christian church. The sweeping technological, sociological, and political changes that have occurred over the 2, 000 years since Christ's birth are impossible to summarize briefly. Much of the world the Christian of today lives in would be beyond the understanding of the Christian living in the Roman and Byzantine empires, during the Middle Ages, or even during the Reformation. Yet that same earlier Christian might enter a Roman Catholic, Eastern Orthodox, or Anglican church and feel quite at home. Similarly, a Protestant of the Reformation would feel comfortable in most contemporary Protestant churches.

Challenges to Christianity today have often come about through the secularization and modernization of society. The increasing worldliness of society has caused at times a decline both in the numbers of some Christian denominations and in the social and political influence of these churches. The secularization of the modern world has also put pressures on the churches to change many of their attitudes. Some have adapted in order to meet these demands and preserve their relevance; others continue to resist.

Christianity in a Secular World

In the Middle Ages, the Christian church of western Europe influenced every aspect of life—family life, work, education, art, and politics. In the 20th century, the sphere of the church's influence has often been narrowed in some countries to its effect on individual and family life. To continue to carry out their mission to the poor, the hungry and the sick, and to spread the gospel of love, Christian churches have had to revitalize their congregations through many new movements.

Ecumenism

One effort to overcome the continual splintering within Christianity and to promote common Christian efforts has been the ecumenical, or church-unity, movement. This movement began in the early decades of the 20th century and for many years was almost exclusively confined to Protestantism. At the international level, the World Council of Churches was formed in Amsterdam, the Netherlands, in 1948. Except for the Roman Catholic church, the council brings together almost all the Christian churches. It works to promote cooperation and unity among all the churches of the world and has opened discussions with non-Christian groups, such as Buddhists and Muslims, as well.

Among the council's united activities are education, missionary work, aid to refugees, and the promotion of world peace. It has studied the role Christians should play in improving government and various social institutions and has sponsored studies on the future of society in an age of scientific and technological progress. On the national level, many Protestant groups have combined and formed new denominations. For example, in the United States, the United Church of Christ brought together Evangelical, Reformed, and Congregational churches. In Canada, Methodists, Congregationalists, and Presbyterians formed the United Church of Canada. The National Council of Churches brings many Protestant groups together to coordinate various activities. The goal of ecumenism is for churches to turn their energies away from defending their denominational boundaries and to begin coming together in prayer and worship as well as in other church activities.

In the 1960s, the Roman Catholic Church began to take a more active part in the ecumenical movement. Among the decrees passed by Vatican II (1962-1965), a worldwide council of Catholic church leaders, was the Decree on Ecumenism. This pledged the Catholic church to work for the unity of all Christianity and encouraged Roman Catholics to take part in the ecumenical movement. The decree also permitted Catholics to join non-Catholics in common prayer, with the permission of local bishops. The Roman Catholic church sees the present goal of the ecumenical movement as being not the creation of a uniform, homogenized church but rather an opportunity for appreciating the different forms of religious expressions.

In 1965, the Roman Catholic church also took a step toward ending the division between itself and Eastern Orthodox churches. On December 7 of that year, Pope Paul VI removed the sentence of excommunication on the patriarch of Constantinople that dated from 1054. The present patriarch of Constantinople in turn removed a sentence of excommunication that the 11th-century patriarch had passed against a group of papal delegates. A decree of Vatican II also reaffirmed the equality of the rites of the Eastern and Western churches and set forth circumstances under which Roman Catholics and Orthodox Christians could participate together in the sacraments and worship.

■ Ecumenism is a movement within Christianity today to foster understanding and cooperation among the various churches. The Greek root for **ecumenism** is **oikoumene**, which means, "the whole world."

The possibility of a reunion between the Catholic and Protestant churches has become more realistic with changes in both faiths. Among other things, Protestants have moved away from the Puritan tradition, and Catholics have ceased to refer to Protestants as heretics. However, although Catholics and Protestants can cooperate in prayer and work, agreement about the basic tenets of the faith must come before there can be any full union. The ecumenical movement, however, has given Christians from many denominations common grounds for developing cooperative energies in today's world.

Charismatic Christianity

Another response to the challenges of a more secular society came in a movement called charismatic Christianity, which stresses personal experience of the Holy Spirit apart from sacraments and church institutions. The movement began with the founding of Pentecostalism in the United States in 1901. Pentecostalism takes its name from the feast of Pentecost, when the apostles experienced the outpouring of the Holy Spirit. Charismatic groups usually meet in houses rather than churches, although prayer meetings may also be held in a church. The meetings are energetic and emotional and include periods of singing, silent meditation, and spontaneous prayer and testimony. There is little if any clerical leadership at charismatic meetings, making the participation of the individual more immediate and vital.

In the 1960s the Jesus movement, a form of charismatic Christianity, became popular among young people. It combined elements of Pentecostalism with features of the way of life of the young, such as the use of rock music in hymns. Another attempt to revive the spirit of Christianity was the "born-again" movement, in which believers reaffirmed their faith in Jesus and experienced that they had been born again into a new and more committed life as Christians. At the core of these charismatic movements has been an attempt to involve the individual in a more immediate and vital way—to make religion more personal and direct. It has tapped new energies in certain Christians by reawakening a more personal faith and by filling a vacuum in societies that have become more and more impersonal and distant.

The Founding of New Religious Denominations

In Europe, the founding of a new church was a conscious act of dissent against the established church of the country. In the United States—which guaranteed freedom of religion and had no established church or orthodox tradition—a new church was the natural outcome of almost any new idea. In 19th-century New York, six persons could constitute a religious society, or church. Consequently, Protestantism has historically divided itself into new groups whenever disagreements arose. Even though this process has often made the two groups weaker, it has at times served to foster renewal that has released new energies. One instance is the establishment of the Progressive National Baptist Convention by Martin Luther King, Jr., in his split from the National Baptist Convention.

Vatican II

On January 25, 1959, Pope John XXIII announced his intention of calling a worldwide church council that would provide an aggiornamento (bringing up to date) of Roman Catholic religious life and teaching. Vatican II, which was opened by Pope John in 1962 and closed by his successor, Pope Paul VI, in 1965, was one of the most widely discussed religious events of the century. Vatican II was important both for the changes it made in Roman Catholicism and for its opening up of discussion and debate. The most important of the documents that came out of Vatican II was the Constitution on the Church. This constitution gave the Roman Catholic bishops throughout the world greater influence in church affairs. By describing the laity and church officials as "members of the people of God" and by not stressing the differences between them, it also gave laypersons a more active part in the Catholic liturgy, or worship service.

Another important reform of the council was the Constitution on the Sacred Liturgy, which permitted, and even encouraged, the use of the vernacular, or local language, in place of Latin in parts of the Mass and in such sacraments as baptism, the Eucharist, and matrimony. This change, as well as revisions in the Mass liturgy itself, opened the way for greater participation by the congregation.

Priesthood and Ministry

The Vatican II Decree on the Ministry and Life of Priests reaffirmed the laws of celibacy for Roman Catholic priests, a subject that draws much attention in discussions today. All other Christian denominations, including the Eastern Orthodox church and the Anglican church, permit married clergy. A large number of Catholic priests leave the priesthood and marry each year, and the number of those preparing for the priesthood has dropped in many regions of the Roman Catholic world, raising concerns that the time will come when there will not be enough priests to serve the Catholic population. The shortage of priests has become more evident in rural areas.

One solution suggested for this problem would be the ordination of women. Traditionally, women have been excluded from the Catholic, Orthodox, and Anglican priesthoods, a condition that exists to this day despite challenges that began with the women's suffrage movement at the turn of the century. In 1853, Antoinette Brown became the first woman minister to be ordained in America. She served a Congregational church in New York State. However, it was a long time before women became ordained in any numbers. The lead in ordination of women was taken by the Lutheran church in Denmark, which ordained three women ministers in 1948. Today, women ministers serve in almost all Protestant denominations.

The ordination of eleven women to the Episcopalian priesthood in 1974 was a crucial step. Because the Episcopal church is a member of the Anglican communion, its theology is Catholic. The acceptance of women into the Episcopalian ministry signals their likely general acceptance in the Anglican communion in the near future.

The refusal of the Catholic church to ordain women is not based on concerns about their ability. The church's argument against the ordination of women is based on the Bible—the fact that Christ was masculine, for example, and that he chose twelve male apostles to carry out his ministry. The Roman Catholic church's position is clearly stated in the Vatican declaration Inter Insigniores (The Order of the Priesthood):

> *This practice of the Church therefore has a normative character; in the fact of conferring priestly ordination only on men, it is a question of the unbroken tradition throughout the history of the Church, universal in the East and in the West, and alert to repress abuses immediately. This norm, based on Christ's example, has been and is still observed because it is considered to conform to God's plan for his Church.*

Birth Control

In the 20th century, faced with the many problems associated with unchecked population growth, such as overcrowding and the danger of spoiling or depleting many of the earth's valuable natural resources, governments have put considerable institutional force behind birth control. With the development of new birth control methods and the desire on the part of many people to limit the size of their families, new challenges have been posed to traditional moral positions of the Christian churches. Although many governments actively encouraged the use of birth control, the entire Christian church remained against it until 1930. In that year, the first significant break in this united Christian front against birth control occurred when the Lambeth Conference of the Anglican church cautiously approved certain methods other than sexual abstinence to avoid parenthood. Between 1930 and 1958 the major Protestant churches all publicly abandoned the absolute prohibition against contraception. By 1959, when the World Council of Churches endorsed contraceptive practice, the Protestant consensus in its favor was very strong. The Orthodox churches of the East and the Roman Catholic church did not alter their position against birth control.

For modern Christians, the issue of birth control is a very complicated one. In making ethical judgments of this kind, moral teachers indicate that it is important to take into account the impact contraception has on society's sexual morals. Does birth control by some individuals promote sexual license and keep love at a shallow level? Or does it reduce fear of pregnancy and thus allow the love between a couple to grow without other concerns? Does contraception foster a disrespect for life in the pursuit of selfish pleasure? Or does it take away tensions in relationships where economic conditions make pregnancy unadvisable? Do governments encourage birth control in cultures and social classes for which they have no respect in order to control undesired population? These and many more complicated questions enter into the debate on contraception. Questions have existed before concerning birth control, but with the new relatively safe and effective technologies and the growing influence that can be exercised by governments, these questions have intensified immensely for Christians in the contemporary world. Many Christians have made the decision to use contraception despite the prohibitive teachings of their church; others have decided to follow church doctrine strictly and refrain from using contraception.

Abortion

Like the issue of birth control, the issue of abortion has taken on grand proportions in the latter part of the 20th century, especially in America. The Second Vatican Council (1965) summarized the commitment of the Catholic church to the welfare of the fetus, condemning abortion as an unspeakable crime and asking that the fetus be given the greatest care right from the moment of conception. Roman Catholic moral teaching does permit the invocation of the "principle of double effect" to argue that in certain extreme situations, such as a threat to the mother's life, the death of the fetus may be permitted (not chosen), because it is not the direct and willful taking of innocent life but rather the indirect result of saving the mother's life. But the Catholic church explicitly denies women a right to choose to terminate an unwanted pregnancy, even in instances of rape or incest, placing a higher value on the life of the fetus than on any such right to choose claimed by women.

Protestant perspectives on the abortion issue vary considerably. At one end of the spectrum, there are the strong anti-abortion voices that, like the Roman Catholics, stress the fetus's right to life, and at the other extreme there are the abortion-on-demand voices that stress the woman's right and freedom to control her own body and its reproductive processes. There are many Protestant positions in between these two extremes, most of them more tolerant of the idea of a woman's right to choose than the Roman Catholic position.

Each pregnancy is unique and is surrounded by its own complex set of issues. Not only religious but medical, economic, and social factors also come into play when a woman is faced with the choice whether to have or not to have an abortion. Consequently, a Christian woman who is considering terminating an unwanted pregnancy must also consider these factors in the light of her moral convictions. Her family, her partner, her doctor, and her priest or minister representing the moral wisdom of her church can provide guidance as she makes the decision. Still, as individuals struggle with the issue of abortion, it remains a controversial issue for Christians in an ever-more-secularized world, with its continually developing medical technology.

■ *Bishop Desmond Tutu, Anglican spiritual leader in South Africa, has fought strongly against apartheid, or segregation, in his native land.*

Religion and Politics

Many moral issues have been considered as exclusively individual moral questions. Today, however, such moral questions as contraception and abortion extend beyond the borders of private morality to include consideration of the social, economic and political conditions that influence an individual's moral decisions. In these and other areas, many Christians have been moved to examine the social and economic conditions under which they live. In the United States, in particular, the Christian churches have, for over a century, seen the need to push for social and political reforms. Despite the separation of church and state and the prohibition of the establishment of any religion, the U.S. Constitution guarantees the right of religious bodies to state their

Liberation theology has given new interpretations to the Gospel of Christ, applying the teaching of Jesus to the poor in South and Central America. Frequently, congregations in these areas of the world celebrate the mass in simple surroundings such as those pictured in this photo.

positions in regard to public policy issues. They cannot constitutionally demand that their positions be legislated as they deem it, but they can try to persuade others concerning the moral correctness of their social and political opinions and attempt to mold public policy.

In recent years, strong Christian movements have marshaled numerous religious forces to appeal to moral values that they believe have grown weak in American society. One such group, the Moral Majority, has backed certain political candidates and lobbied Congress and the White House in order to further its moral political agenda. Efforts on the part of such Christian groups are frequently judged by secularists to be extreme and disrespectful of the rights of people to live life as they choose.

When strong religious and political forces combine, there often results such strong conviction of rightness that objective discussion of issues can be diminished. Moderation and toleration can give way to fanaticism when religion and politics mix. When people feel threatened by the intensity of this conviction, as they often do, they tend not only to oppose the political positions associated with these groups but also the churches that have become too identified with those positions. Most of these religious movements, however, have not taken on fanatical form. For the most part they continue to make valuable contributions to the moral, social, and political debates that take place in democracies every day.

Liberation Theology

In South and Central America the interplay of politics and religion has been the focus of much attention since the time of the Second Vatican Council (1965). Vatican II called on Catholics to be engaged in the modern world and its problems. The social situations in many South and Central American countries was such that 90 percent of the people were counted among the poor. In 1968, the Catholic bishops of South America called on all Catholics to become involved in social questions. They also declared that the church should give special consideration to the poor.

In 1972, this call of the Catholic bishops found expression in Gustavo Guttierez's book *A Theology of Liberation*. The work of this Peruvian priest began the movement called liberation theology. The chief characteristic of this movement is that it understands the church's gospel message of freedom to be one that is interpreted in view of the experience of the poor and the oppressed. The leading teachers of this movement have been Leonardo and Clodovis Boff in Brazil and Jon Sobrino, a Mexican priest, in El Salvador.

The liberation theology movement has had significant success in focusing attention on the plight of the poor and has pulled together efforts to alleviate their suffering. At times this movement has been painted, by its foes, as Marxist and as opposed to

United States interests. Indeed, leading voices of liberation theology have been critical of the capitalist system, which they believe exploits and ignores the poor.

Efforts at progress in improving the social lot of the poor in South and Central America have not always been peaceful. In 1989, six Jesuit priests, and their housekeeper and her daughter, were murdered in El Salvador while some of them were engaged in negotiations between the government and warring guerillas.

In these efforts, the Christian churches have moved into new and more delicate roles in different societies. Its judgments, discretion, prudence, and courage are tested in new and politically complicated ways. However, that they make these efforts shows that the Christian churches are still alive and active in the contemporary world, struggling with its technological, economic, political, and social problems.

Conclusion

Christianity is currently under siege by both worldliness and secularism. The churches, however, have proved resilient. The many continuing activities of the Christian churches in today's world—their life of prayer, their many forms of renewal, their charismatic revivals, their reawakening in eastern Europe, their growth in Africa, their new commitments in South and Central America, and their ecumenical generosity—suggest that the promise of Christ at the end of Matthew's Gospel is still being fulfilled: "Go, then, to all people everywhere and make them my disciples. . . . I will be with you always, to the end of the world." (Matt. 28.19-20)

GLOSSARY

Catechism—A textbook of questions and answers regarding Christian beliefs and life used for preparing Catholics to accept the responsibilities of mature faith demanded by the sacrament of confirmation.

Charismatic movements—A religious movement, begun as Pentecostalism in the United States in 1901, that accentuates personal and direct experience of the Holy Spirit independently of sacraments and church institutions.

Chrism—Holy oil blessed for confirmation and symbolizing the strength that is necessary for leading a mature Christian life and facing the challenges the call to Christian maturity brings.

Christening—The formal naming of an infant that often takes place at baptism. The name taken is usually that of a saintly person whom one can look upon as a model and inspiration for her or his life.

College of cardinals—A group of Catholics, usually clergymen, who are appointed by the pope to serve as his advisers. Their main task is to elect a successor to a deceased pope.

Creed—A short statement of the basic beliefs of the Christian church (e.g. the Apostles' Creed, the Athanasian Creed, and the Nicene Creed).

Epiphany—Feast celebrated on January 6 that commemorates the manifestation of Christ to the Gentiles in the persons of the Magi.

Excommunication—The formal cutting off of a person from the life of the church and the reception of the sacraments.

Fathers of the church—Early church authors (e.g., Ambrose, Jerome, Augustine, Basil, Gregory the Great) who explained the Scriptures with great acuity and whose writings thus gained authority within the church community.

Final Judgment—In contrast to the particular judgment given at death, this is the time, at Christ's Second Coming, when the fate of human beings will be decided for all eternity.

Icons—Representations in paint or enamel of sacred personages, such as Christ or the saints, that are themselves venerated and considered sacred, especially in the Orthodox churches.

Incarnation—The mystery believed by Christians that God became man by the union of his divine and human natures in the person of Jesus Christ.

Infallibility—The belief held by Roman Catholics that the pope cannot make an error in matters of faith and morals when he speaks by virtue of his office.

Judaizers—Those Christians in the early church who favored a more Jewish form of Christianity that would require all converts to Christ to become circumcised. Saint Paul refers to them as "members of the circumcision party."

Messiah—An anointed king promised to the Jewish people as someone who would lead them to overcome their enemies. Messiah, in Hebrew, means "anointed one." The corresponding word in Greek is Christos, or, in English, "Christ."

Monk—A religious man following the Rule of Saint Benedict who spends most of his day in prayer and who attempts to lead a perfect Christian life by taking vows pledging himself to poverty, chastity, and obedience.

Novena—Roman Catholic devotions consisting of prayers or services held on nine consecutive days or weeks honoring Mary, the mother of Jesus, or the saints.

Pentecost—Feast celebrated by Christian believers, commemorating Christ's sending of the Holy Spirit to the apostles. It is considered by Christians to be the birthday of the church.

Plainsong—A simple melody sung without instrumental accompaniment or harmony that developed gradually from early Jewish religious music. The most famous form of plainsong is the Gregorian chant developed during the reign of Pope Gregory I.

Protestant—A term first used in 1529 to express the protest of several princes of fourteen German cities against an attempt by the Roman Catholic emperor Charles V to end the practice of Lutheranism within the Holy Roman Empire. The term later was extended to Lutherans and other Christians who separated from Roman Catholicism.

Roman curia—The group that serves as the pope's administrative arm. It consists of the secretariat of state, which assists the pope most directly in governing the church, and a number of other departments, each of which has a specific function.

Sacraments—Signs of divine help or grace, needed for living a good Christian life, through which God confers the help or grace he promises.

Schism—A split between two churches that does not involve the denial of any truth of the faith. Such a denial of a truth of the Christian faith would be called heresy.

Second Vatican Council—A worldwide church council for Roman Catholics opened by Pope John XXIII in 1962 for bringing Roman Catholic life and teaching up to date. Vatican II was closed by Pope Paul VI in 1965.

Seminary—A school for training members of the clergy for most denominations of Christians.

Trinity—The Christian belief that in God there are three persons: the Father, the Son (who became man in Christ), and the Holy Spirit.

Vernacular—Local language permitted to be used in religious ceremonies instead of the official Latin language that had been used by Catholics for centuries. Also the language employed by Luther in making the Bible more avail-

FOR FURTHER READING

Bainton, Roland, and the Editors of *Horizon* magazine. *The Horizon History of Christianity*. New York: American Heritage Publishing Co., 1964.

Brown, Schuyler. *The Origins of Christianity: A Historical Introduction to the New Testament*. New York: Oxford University Press, 1984.

Gibbon, Edward. *The Early Growth of Christianity and the History of the First Christians*. American Classical College Press, 1986.

Green, Michael. *What Is Christianity?* Nashville: Abingdon, 1982.

Johnson, Paul. *A History of Christianity*. New York: Macmillan, 1976.

Lewis, C. S. *The Case for Christianity*. New York: Macmillan, 1943.

Marty, Martin E. *Christianity in the New World: From 1500-1800*. Houston: Harper, 1984.

Peters, F. E. *Judaism, Christianity, and Islam: The Classical Texts and Their Interrpretation*. Princeton: Princeton University Press, 1990.

Russell, D. S. *From Early Judaism to Early Church*. Minneapolis: Augsburg Fortress, 1986.

Schaff, Philip. *History of the Christian Church*. (8 volumes) Grand Rapids: Eerdman's, 1960.

INDEX

Pentecost Sunday. *see* Anglicanism, observances of; Eastern Orthodoxy, observances of; Protestantism, observances of; Roman Catholicism observances of
Pharisees 25, 26, 27, 28, 29
Plainsong 103
Pontius Pilate 29, 31
Presbyterian Church 8, 13, 70, 112
Priesthood 88, 115-116
Priests 59, 96
Progressive National Baptist Convention 114
Protestantism 11, 45, 48, 62-74, 81, 113, 114, 116, 117, 118; beliefs of 62-71; early churches of 64-71; Lutherans 65-67; Anabaptists 67-78; Calvinism 68-71; Methodism 71-72; worship of 72-73; church organization of 73; observances of 73-74
Purgatory 50
Puritans 70, 109, 113

Quakers 8, 15, 73, 82, 87

Reconciliation 53
Reformation 42, 48, 71, 97, 101, 102, 109, 112
Reformed churches 70, 112

Resurrection of Jesus. *see* Jesus Christ, resurrection of
Roman Catholicism 8, 11, 44, 45, 48, 51, 59, 64, 67, 75, 81, 83, 88, 90, 97, 110, 112, 113, 117; beliefs of 48-51, 58; worship of 51-54; church organization of 54-55, 115; observances of 55-57; weddings 87

Sacramentals 52
Sacraments 52-54
Saint Mary the Virgin. *see* Anglicanism, observances of
Saints Peter and Paul 62, 77. *see also* Anglicanism, observances of; Eastern Orthodoxy, observances of
Second Vatican Council. *see* Vatican II
Seminary 11, 88
Sermon on the Mount 25, 37
Seven sacraments (of the Roman Catholic church) 52-54
Seventh-day Adventists 8, 95
Simons, Menno 68, 77. *see also* Mennonites
Sistine Chapel 101, 102
Smith, Joseph 77
Society of Friends 73. *see also* Quakers
Sunday of Orthodoxy 62. *see*

also Eastern Orthodoxy, observances of

Temple, The 23, 27, 28
Ten Commandments 18, 25
Transfiguration of Jesus Christ 63. *see also* Eastern Orthodoxy, observances of
Trinity 48, 49, 50, 53, 55, 57, 84
Tutu, Bishop Desmond 13

Unitarians 8
United Church of Christ 112
United Lutheran Church 12, 67
United Synod South 12

Vatican II 52, 115, 118, 121
Vincent de Paul 40
Virgin Mary. *see* Mary (mother of Jesus Christ)

Waite, Terry 13
Wesley, Charles 71
Wesley, John 71, 77
World Council of Chruches 11, 112, 117

Zwingli, Ulrich 43, 67, 77